ALPHA
AND OMEGA
MALE

ALPHA
AND OMEGA
MALE
Savior Provocateur

Mike VanOuse

Copyright © 2020 Mike VanOuse

All rights reserved

ISBN: 978-1-7342702-6-6

Table of Contents

1. Connecting the Dots..1
2. I AM...7
3. Escalate..11
4. Born Blind..15
5. Allegory...21
6. Shepherd..23
7. Condemned..27
8. Matthew...31
9. Mark..37
10. Luke..39
11. Simmer to Boil..43
12. Boil...49
13. Yoke...53
14. SuperMan..59
15. Supermen..63
16. Stealth..69
17. Tough Guys..73
18. Saul..79
19. Return...85
20. References..91

1. Connecting the Dots

In John Chapter 1, Jesus is introduced to the world as the Word of God made flesh[1], was baptized by John, and began collecting disciples.

In Chapter 2, He turned water into wine (first miracle)[2], went to the Passover in Jerusalem, made a whip of cords and drove the money-changers out of the temple. This initiated His contention with the religious officials.

In Chapter 3, He explained to Nicodemus that a man must be born again to see the Kingdom of God, reciting verse16 – "For God so loved the world…"

In Chapter 4, Jesus offered the Samaritan woman at the well living water[3], and told her that He is the Messiah Who is to come[4].

In Chapter 5, He made the religious officials angry enough to kill Him by healing a man on the Sabbath and claiming to be equal with God[5].

In Chapter 6, He miraculously fed thousands of people, who then followed Him for more free stuff. He rebuked them and said things so difficult to comprehend, many abandoned Him[6].

In Chapter 7, He attended the Jewish Feast of the Tabernacles in Jerusalem, and taught openly in the Temple, which surprised many, because everyone knew that the religious officials wanted to kill Him[7].

John 7:
> 37 *In the last day, that great [day] of the feast, Jesus stood and cried, saying, If any man thirst, let him come unto me, and drink.*
> 38 *He that believeth on me, as the scripture hath said, out of his belly shall flow rivers of living water.*
> 39 *(But this spake he of the Spirit, which they that believe on him should receive: for the Holy Ghost was not yet [given;] because that Jesus was not yet glorified.)*

For a cursory reader of the New Testament, this seems like a very cryptic thing to say. Why did He say it, and what did He mean?

---

1. John 1:1, 14
2. John 2:11
3. John 4:10
4. John 4:25-26
5. John 5:18
6. John 6:66 (ironic number for the rejection of Christ.)
7. John 7:25

There were 3 annual feasts in Israel: The Day of Atonement, Passover, and the Feast of Tabernacles. He said this during the Feast of Tabernacles, which is also called the Feast of the Ingathering, because it occurs at the end of the harvest season, just before the rainy season.

There were daily sacrifices performed at the Temple, and monthly sacrifices, each including a wine libation poured on the alter with the sacrifice. What made the Feast of Tabernacles unique was that the daily sacrifices included a water libation called "Nisuch ha-Mayim," to invoke God's blessing on the rains.

The prelude to Nisuch ha-Mayim was a ritual where the priests would go down to the pool of Siloam to draw the water for the ritual, called, "the rejoicing of the house of water-drawing," or "Simchat Beit Hashoeivah."

One of the scriptures referenced during the festival was Isaiah 12:3

Isaiah 12:
> 3 *Therefore with joy shall ye draw water out of the wells of salvation.*

Of the 3 annual feasts, the Feast of Tabernacles was the facsimile of New-Year's Eve in Times Square. Since the priests drew the water out of the pool of Siloam at dawn, and Isaiah said to do it with joy: The Israelites partied all night beforehand, with music, dancing and torches, as a prelude.

It was the most festive event on the Hebrew calendar. That's the historical backdrop to John 7:37:

John 7:
> 37 *In the last day, that great [day] of the feast, Jesus stood and cried, saying, If any man thirst, let him come unto me, and drink.*

The praises they sang during the feast were called the Hallel: Psalms 113-118. All those psalms lauded the Messiah who was to come.

When Jesus stood and made His announcement, He was saying, "This entire festival is celebrating the arrival of the Messiah – it's ME! Come to Me!"

It's not obvious to the modern reader, but it was in-your-face blatant to the audience He delivered it to.

Why is that significant? Because it's the segue to John Chapter 8, where they brought the woman caught in the act of adultery before Jesus.

John 8:
> 3 *And the scribes and Pharisees brought unto him a woman taken in adultery; and when they had set her in the midst,*
> 4 *They say unto him, Master, this woman was taken in adultery, in the very act.*
> 5 *Now Moses in the law commanded us, that such should be stoned: but what sayest thou?*
> 6 *This they said, tempting him, that they might have to accuse him. But Jesus stooped down, and with [his] finger wrote on the ground, [as though he heard them not.]*
> 7 *So when they continued asking him, he lifted up himself, and said unto them, He that is without sin among you, let him first cast a stone at her.*
> 8 *And again he stooped down, and wrote on the ground.*
> 9 *And they which heard [it,] being convicted by [their own] conscience, went out one by one, beginning at the eldest, [even] unto the last: and Jesus was left alone, and the woman standing in the midst.*
> 10 *When Jesus had lifted up himself, and saw none but the woman, he said unto her, Woman, where are those thine accusers? hath no man condemned thee?*
> 11 *She said, No man, Lord. And Jesus said unto her, Neither do I condemn thee: go, and sin no more.*

He stooped down and wrote on the ground. What did He write? It doesn't say. Many a sermon has conceded that "we don't know." Maybe we do.

This is where the significance of John 7, with Jesus declaring at the Feast of Tabernacles that if any man thirsts, come to Him and drink, applies:

Jeremiah 17:
> 13 *O LORD, the hope of Israel, all that forsake thee shall be ashamed, [and] they that depart from me shall be written in the earth, because they have forsaken the LORD, the fountain of living waters.*

Jesus had just declared Himself to be the fountain of living waters. Then, when confronted with the woman caught in adultery, He stooped down and wrote in the earth. And when He did, those that were ashamed turned away.

He wrote their names in the dirt.

Is that a cool teaching, or what? I wish I could take credit for it, or give credit to whoever came up with it, but I heard it 20-some-years-ago from a friend who heard it from another. I did do the footwork to look up the rites of the Feast of Tabernacles to substantiate it, but someone more scholarly than I connected the dots and put it all together. May God bless them richly.

Put yourself for a moment in the shoes of the woman's accusers: Some yokel comes to your town preaching outlandish stuff. You and your buddies who have never met him decide to put him to the test. When he writes your name in the dirt, you would have to think to yourself, "What else does he know?"

The golden rule of hermeneutics – the science of scripture interpretation – is that man does not interpret scripture: scripture interprets scripture. So if you wish to be dogmatic about a theological postulation, you must come up with corroborating scriptures to back-up what you have to say.

One scripture isn't enough to establish doctrine:

2 Corinthians 13:
> 1 *This is the third time I am coming to you. In the mouth of two or three witnesses shall every word be established.*

Deuteronomy 17:
> 6 *At the mouth of two witnesses, or three witnesses, shall he that is worthy of death be put to death; but at the mouth of one witness he shall not be put to death.*

Since the Jeremiah 17 reference is an obscure passage, you can't be dogmatic about saying it was the names of the accusers that Jesus wrote in the dirt. It's a sound bet if you want to put money on it though.

But that insight into the incident is by no means the summation of glory revealed in it. The scribes and Pharisees brought a beautiful woman before Jesus accusing her of a crime that the law said was punishable by death and asked Him His position.

The object was to provoke Him to contradict the Law of Moses with His answer[8]. He didn't answer. But by the time He got done scribbling in the dirt, all of her accusers had left.

John 8:

---

8   John 8:6

> 10 *When Jesus had lifted up himself, and saw none but the woman, he said unto her, Woman, where are those thine accusers? hath no man condemned thee?*
> 11 *She said, No man, Lord. And Jesus said unto her, Neither do I condemn thee: go, and sin no more.*

It requires the testimony of two or three witnesses to condemn someone to death according to the Law of Moses. Whatever Jesus wrote in the dirt, it caused all of her accusers to vacate. According to the Law, she could not be put to death in the absence of accusers.

And He didn't have to contradict the Law to accomplish that.

There is so much glory buried in that chapter of scripture it's breath-taking. His response to her accusers was:

John 8:

> 7 ...*He that is without sin among you, let him first cast a stone at her.*

That intimates that there is no one without sin. But in truth, there was one among them who was without sin: Himself.

You could paraphrase that passage as, "I get to throw the first rock."

And He threw it at them.

Glory to God.

Alpha & Omega MALE

2. I AM

The Old Testament contains several names of God. In Genesis 1:1, it's El-Ohim (אֱלֹהִים)[9], which is more of a title than a name. It's actually the plural form of Eloi (אֱלוֹהַּ)[10]. You may recall Jesus' cry from the cross, *"Eloi, Eloi, lama sabachthani?*[11]*" "My God, My God, why hast thou forsaken Me?"*

El (אל) is a generic form of God. You find it in a lot of biblical names. The name, Isra-el (יִשְׂרָאֵל) translates to, "wrestles with God[12]." "Samu-el" (שְׁמוּאֵל) means "asked of God[13]."

El Shaddai (אל שדי) means, "God Almighty."

Then there's Jehovah. When Moses met God at the burning-bush, part of the dialog goes as follows:

> Exodus 3:
> 13 *And Moses said unto God, Behold, when I come unto the children of Israel, and shall say unto them, The God of your fathers hath sent me unto you; and they shall say to me, What is his name? what shall I say unto them?*
> 14 *And God said unto Moses, I AM THAT I AM: and he said, Thus shalt thou say unto the children of Israel, I AM hath sent me unto you.*
> 15 *And God said moreover unto Moses, Thus shalt thou say unto the children of Israel, The LORD God of your fathers, the God of Abraham, the God of Isaac, and the God of Jacob, hath sent me unto you: this is my name for ever, and this is my memorial unto all generations.*

In verse 15, the word, "LORD" in the original Hebrew manuscripts is, YHWH (יְהֹוָה)[14], called in theological circles, the "tetragrammaton." The letters in the Hebrew alphabet (or alephbet) are pronounced, "yod-he-vad-he." The definition is: "the existing One," or, "HE IS."

---

9 Strong's Comprehensive Concordance, H430
10 Strong's H433
11 Mark 15:34
12 Strong's H3478
13 Strong's H8050
14 Strong's H3068

That is where the word transliterated into English, "Jehovah" comes from. Notice, there are only 4 letters in the word. How did we get a 7-letter word out of that in English?

In giving the 10 Commandments, God told Moses that thou shalt not take the Name of the Lord thy God in vain[15]. After the Babylonian captivity, the Jews took that commandment so literally, that in reading scriptures aloud, when they would come to the tetragrammaton, they would not pronounce it. Instead, they would insert the word, "Lord," so as not to speak it in vain.

"Lord," in Hebrew, is "Adonai" (אֲדֹנָי)[16].

The original Hebrew alephbet contained no vowels. In the 12th century, a group of rabbis called the Masoretes added vowel characters to the Hebrew alephbet, inserting the vowels from "Adonai" between the consonants of "YHWH." When translating the masoretic text into English, translators came up with the word, "Jehovah."

Following suit to the Jewish tradition, when translating "YHWH" into English, instead of transcribing "Jehovah," they inserted, "LORD." When reading an English translation of the Old Testament, if the last 3 letters in "Lord" are lower case, the original word in Hebrew was "Adon," or "Adonai." If the last 3 letters are small caps, the original was "YHWH."

The Jews went so many centuries without pronouncing the tetragrammaton in its original form that the pronunciation of it is now obscure. Many denominations of Christianity choose to pronounce it, "Yah-weh," discarding the masoretic vowels.

Often times in the Old Testament, God would deliver one of the patriarchs from some trial, and out of gratitude, they would build an altar and name it according to the deliverance they just experienced.

Par exemple, When Abraham was going to sacrifice Isaac on Mount Moriah and God provided a ram as a substitute, Abraham named the place, "Jehovahjireh[17]."

Modern study guides will tell you that this translates as, "The LORD our Provider." Other examples include but are not limited to:
Jehovah-Elohim = The LORD our God
Jehovah-Adonai = The LORD our Lord

---

15 Exodus 20:7
16 Strong's Comprehensive Concordance H113
17 Geneis 22:14

Jehovah-Rophe = The LORD our Healer
Jehovah-Nissi = The LORD our Banner
Jehovah-Sabaoth = The LORD of Hosts
Etc. (an Internet search for biblical names of god will provide the rest.)

This isn't surface teaching: Many church-goers will reference a name of God from that list in the Old Testament when focusing on a particular aspect of the multi-faceted character of God.

What frustrates me is that "Jehovah," or "Yah-weh," or "YHWH" doesn't translate to, "LORD." That's "Adonai." Again, YHWH translates to, "the existent One," or rather, "HE IS."

What all those Old Testament names of God translate to are more accurately:
He IS our Provider.
He IS our Lord.
He IS our Healer.
Etc.

Do you see the difference? It's subtle, but significant. It's personal to Him: It's not a title – i.e. "the Boss, our Source" – it's a statement of fact just as His proper Name is: HE IS our Source.

Returning to Moses dialoguing with the Burning Bush, God first answers Moses' inquiry into His name with, "I AM[18]." "Hayah" (הָיָה) in Hebrew[19].

Two Names, same Deity: if we invoke the sacred Name of God, it translates to, "HE IS." But it would be improper for Him to use that moniker. So when He invokes His own Name, it's "I AM." More than a Name, it's a Truth-statement.

---

18   Exodus 3:14
19   Strong's Comprehensive Concordance H1961

3. Escalate

Fallen human nature is impervious to ethnic distinctions. Some who have presented the Gospel have been accused of being anti-Semitic because they cast the "Jews" in a negative light. But the Jews are no different in nature to any other race of the descendants of Adam.

When the Gospel casts the Jews in a negative light, it is speaking specifically of the authorities in the Jewish religion of the period. In every microcosm of humanity, there are power-hungry, greedy, proud people who gravitate to positions of authority to exploit those subject to them. It's not a uniquely Jewish thing. The Gospel applies to all humanity.

(The Bible casts some of the Jewish religious leaders of the period in a favorable light, i.e.: Nicodemus[20], Joseph of Arimathea[21], Gamaliel[22].)

After being frustrated in their efforts to catch Jesus contradicting the Law of Moses with the woman caught in the act, the Jews began contending with Him as He taught. Anyone schooled in rhetoric can get good grades on the debate team, but you have to be really gifted to debate with God[23].

So when they challenged His Excellency from on High with pedantic accusations from scripture, not only did He addle their brains with esoteric responses, but He also threw in a few barbs to prick their pride.

> John 8:
> 23 *And he said unto them, Ye are from beneath; I am from above: ye are of this world; I am not of this world.*
> 24 *I said therefore unto you, that ye shall die in your sins: for if ye believe not that I am [he,] ye shall die in your sins.*

Not an answer, He threw that one in at no additional cost as an "FYI."

Notice in verse 24 when He said, *"if ye believe not that I am [he,],"* the word "he," is in brackets. That means that it was added by translators for clarity. What he actually said in the original Greek manuscripts was, *"if ye believe not that I am, ye shall die in your sins."*

"I AM" is what the Jews hallow as the sacred Name of God[24].

---

20 John 3:1-2, 7:50-51
21 John 19:38
22 Acts 5:35-40
23 Job 39:1-2
24 Exodus 3:14

Those 2 verses: John 8:23-24, were a verbal bayonet assault: Lunge, twist, kick, extract. *"I am from above; Ye are from beneath; Ye shall die in your sins; I AM."* It was intended to infuriate them and it prospered. Continued:

> John 8:
> 44 *Ye are of your father the devil, and the lusts of [your] father ye will do. He was a murderer from the beginning, and abode not in the truth, because there is no truth in him. When he speaketh a lie, he speaketh of his own: for he is a liar, and the father of it.*

Again, not a direct answer to a question, Jesus nonchalantly informs them that they're liars, murderers and children of the devil. That's always a good way to break the ice in a conversation: Re: *"How to win friends and influence people."* The Pharisees:

> John 8:
> 53 *Art thou greater than our father Abraham, which is dead? and the prophets are dead: whom makest thou thyself?*
> 54 *Jesus answered, If I honour myself, my honour is nothing: it is my Father that honoureth me; of whom ye say, that he is your God:*

(Jesus rarely answered questions directly. When the woman at the well asked if He was greater than our father Jacob[25], He could have shrugged and said, *"Yeah."* But He didn't. When the Pharisees asked, *"Art thou greater than our father Abraham,"* He could have said, *"Way-more."* When they asked, *"Whom makest thyself?"* He could have said, *"I didn't make myself. My Father, whom ye call God, begat Me."*) Jesus, continued:

> John 8:
> 55 *Yet ye have not known him; but I know him: and if I should say, I know him not, I shall be a liar like unto you: but I know him, and keep his saying.*

He called them liars again. Twist. Jesus, continued:

> John 8:;
> 56 *Your father Abraham rejoiced to see my day: and he saw [it,] and was glad.*
> 57 *Then said the Jews unto him, Thou art not yet fifty years old, and hast thou seen Abraham?*

---

25 John 4:12

> 58 *Jesus said unto them, Verily, verily, I say unto you, Before Abraham was, I am.*
> 59 *Then took they up stones to cast at him: but Jesus hid himself, and went out of the temple, going through the midst of them, and so passed by.*

There's that "I AM" statement again. Twist.

The religiocrites of the day loved being seen in public wearing long, flowing holy garments with all their fringes and phylacteries. They loved being called, "Rabbi" and being seated in the prominent places during gatherings[26]. They loved being considered the authorities in the ways of holiness.

Exercising their authority, they confront an uneducated carpenter in a humble tunic. Instead of bowing to their magnificence, He calmly tells them that they're children of the devil, liars and murderers, and that they'll die in sin. Then He punctuates it with, *"Oh yeah, and I am your God."* In public.

(*That actually concludes this chapter as to Jesus provoking the religiocrites to anger. But if you've ever pondered the verses that say that God hardened Pharaoh's heart[27] so that he wouldn't let the children of Israel go, this is how He did it. He did not manipulate Pharaoh. Pharaoh sat on his throne in all of his magnificent splendor, and a humble shepherd in dirty clothes showed up giving him orders: "Let my people go." It pricked his pride.*)

Per Chapter 5, the pharisees were already offended enough to kill Jesus[28]. This dialog was only included to intensify their indignation and seal His fate.

---

26   Matthew 23:5-7
27   Exodus 4:21
28   John 5:18

Alpha & Omega MALE

4. Born Blind

John Chapter 8 closed with:

> 59 *Then took they up stones to cast at him: but Jesus hid himself, and went out of the temple, going through the midst of them, and so passed by.*

I don't know how you hide yourself in the "*midst of them.*" Nevertheless, He passed by. That brings us to:

> John 9
> 1 *And as [Jesus] passed by, he saw a man which was blind from [his] birth.*
> 2 *And his disciples asked him, saying, Master, who did sin, this man, or his parents, that he was born blind?*
> 3 *Jesus answered, Neither hath this man sinned, nor his parents: but that the works of God should be made manifest in him.*

I've read many allusions to this passage that criticize the disciples for their superstitious assumption that the infirmity was due to sin, as though they were rubes. They weren't. They accompanied Jesus during His ministry and witnessed Him saying things like:

> Matthew 9:
> 5 *For whether is easier, to say, Thy sins be forgiven thee; or to say, Arise, and walk?*

Based on Jesus' own example, it was rational to associate infirmity with sin. Let's continue:

> John 9:
> 4 *I must work the works of him that sent me, while it is day: the night cometh, when no man can work.*
> 5 *As long as I am in the world, I am the light of the world.*
> 6 *When he had thus spoken, he spat on the ground, and made clay of the spittle, and he anointed the eyes of the blind man with the clay,*
> 7 *And said unto him, Go, wash in the pool of Siloam, (which is by interpretation, Sent.) He went his way therefore, and washed, and came seeing.*

All miracles are unique, or they wouldn't be considered miracles. This one was unique in more than one way. As the beneficiary of the miracle testifies later in the chapter, no one in the history of the world who was born blind had ever received their sight before.

In his writings, faith-healer John G. Lake (1870-1935) pointed out that this was not a healing: A healing is when something was healthy, became broken, and was repaired. The man in John 9 never had healthy eyes. He may not even have had eyes. This was a "creation" miracle.

Man was created from the dust of the earth[29]. Jesus took substance from Himself, mixed it with earth and added it to the man. The clay became eyes. John Chapter 1 tells us, *"All things were made by him; and without him was not any thing made that was made[30]."* Nothing new for Jesus.

Creation began with the command, "Let there be light[31]." On the seventh day, God ended His work[32]. Jesus prefaced creating the man's new eyes by stating that He needed to *"work the works of him that sent me,"* then proclaimed Himself to be the "Light of the world." He was thereby revealing this event as a creation work.

Let's return to the story for the aftermath of this creation.

> John 9:
> 8 *The neighbours therefore, and they which before had seen him that he was blind, said, Is not this he that sat and begged?*
> 9 *Some said, This is he: others [said,] He is like him: [but] he said, I am [he.]*
> 10 *Therefore said they unto him, How were thine eyes opened?*
> 11 *He answered and said, A man that is called Jesus made clay, and anointed mine eyes, and said unto me, Go to the pool of Siloam, and wash: and I went and washed, and I received sight.*
> 12 *Then said they unto him, Where is he? He said, I know not.*

Of course he didn't know. He was still blind the last time he had contact with Jesus. This guy didn't have any idea what He looked like: He never saw Him. Jesus could have been standing in front of him, and he still wouldn't have known where He was. Continued:

> John 9:
> 13 *They brought to the Pharisees him that aforetime was blind.*
> 14 *And it was the sabbath day when Jesus made the clay, and opened his eyes.*

---

29 Genesis 2:7
30 John 1:3
31 Genesis 1:3
32 Genesis 2:2

15 Then again the Pharisees also asked him how he had received his sight. He said unto them, He put clay upon mine eyes, and I washed, and do see.
16 Therefore said some of the Pharisees, This man is not of God, because he keepeth not the sabbath day. Others said, How can a man that is a sinner do such miracles? And there was a division among them.
17 They say unto the blind man again, What sayest thou of him, that he hath opened thine eyes? He said, He is a prophet.
18 But the Jews did not believe concerning him, that he had been blind, and received his sight, until they called the parents of him that had received his sight.
19 And they asked them, saying, Is this your son, who ye say was born blind? how then doth he now see?
20 His parents answered them and said, We know that this is our son, and that he was born blind:
21 But by what means he now seeth, we know not; or who hath opened his eyes, we know not: he is of age; ask him: he shall speak for himself.
22 These [words] spake his parents, because they feared the Jews: for the Jews had agreed already, that if any man did confess that he was Christ, he should be put out of the synagogue.
23 Therefore said his parents, He is of age; ask him.

These guys wielded the bludgeon of political correctness. The Romans ran the government, but the Jewish officials controlled the culture.

> John 9:
> *24 Then again called they the man that was blind, and said unto him, Give God the praise: we know that this man is a sinner.*
> *25 He answered and said, Whether he be a sinner [or no,] I know not: one thing I know, that, whereas I was blind, now I see.*
> *26 Then said they to him again, What did he to thee? how opened he thine eyes?*
> *27 He answered them, I have told you already, and ye did not hear: wherefore would ye hear [it] again? will ye also be his disciples?*
> *28 Then they reviled him, and said, Thou art his disciple; but we are Moses' disciples.*
> *29 We know that God spake unto Moses: [as for] this [fellow,] we know not from whence he is.*
> *30 The man answered and said unto them, Why herein is a marvellous thing, that ye know not from whence he is, and [yet] he hath opened mine eyes.*

> 31 *Now we know that God heareth not sinners: but if any man be a worshipper of God, and doeth his will, him he heareth.*
> 32 *Since the world began was it not heard that any man opened the eyes of one that was born blind.*
> 33 *If this man were not of God, he could do nothing.*

In verse 24, they, being the authorities, ordered the man born blind to, *"Give God the praise."* He complied. So they *"reviled"* him. There are some people whom you just can't make happy.

I love this guy. Everyone else – even his parents – cowered in fear of the retribution the Pharisees could foist upon them. He didn't. He didn't care what kind of flowery robes they were wearing, or what their lofty titles were. He spoke truth to power and lipped-off with, *"will ye also be his disciples?"*

Assuming my faith endures to the end, I'll meet this guy in glory.

> John 9:
> 34 *They answered and said unto him, Thou wast altogether born in sins, and dost thou teach us? And they cast him out.*
> 35 *Jesus heard that they had cast him out; and when he had found him, he said unto him, Dost thou believe on the Son of God?*
> 36 *He answered and said, Who is he, Lord, that I might believe on him?*
> 37 *And Jesus said unto him, Thou hast both seen him, and it is he that talketh with thee.*
> 38 *And he said, Lord, I believe. And he worshipped him.*
> 39 *And Jesus said, For judgment I am come into this world, that they which see not might see; and that they which see might be made blind.*
> 40 *And [some] of the Pharisees which were with him heard these words, and said unto him, Are we blind also?*
> 41 *Jesus said unto them, If ye were blind, ye should have no sin: but now ye say, We see; therefore your sin remaineth.*

When Jesus heard they had cast him out, He stopped what He was doing and looked him up. Now that the guy had glorified Him sight-unseen, Jesus made special effort to reveal Himself to him and be seen. He rewards those who serve His purposes, going out of His way to do so.

From the beginning of His ministry, the religious officials perceived Jesus as a threat to the control they wielded over the masses. In John 5 they sought to kill Him for not following the rules. In John 7 He announced that He Is the fountain of living water they were celebrating.

In John 8 He flat-out said, "I AM," further infuriating them. And in John 9, while they still had the rocks in their hands to stone Him, He proved it by performing a creation miracle.

For all this, He still wasn't finished with them yet.

5. Allegory

John, Tom, and James
JOHN was a bad boy, and beat a poor cat;
Tom put a stone in a blind man's hat;
James was the boy who neglected his prayers;
They've all grown up ugly, and nobody cares[33].

This is a digression, but while the man born blind in John Chapter 9 is fresh in your mind is the appropriate time to insert it.

When I read the above poem years ago, I said, "What's the deal with putting a stone in a blind man's hat?" Someone answered, "Blind men sit street-side with their hat on the ground for benevolent passersby to throw coins into. Once there's an accumulation, you can throw a rock in it, causing a 'ching,' tricking him into getting his hopes up that he's getting more."

> Leviticus 19:
> 14 *Thou shalt not curse the deaf, nor put a stumblingblock before the blind, but shalt fear thy God: I [am] the LORD.*

It's an act of cruelty and of irreverence toward God.

> Deuteronomy 27:
> 18 *Cursed [be] he that maketh the blind to wander out of the way. And all the people shall say, Amen.*

There is an invisible realm surrounding us inhabited by spirits. There are angels, both holy and fallen, and demons. Except on rare occasions when the veil is lifted, we cannot see them[34]. In this respect, we are all born blind.

The evil ones play tricks on us; making us to wander out of the way, laying temptations before us to get our hopes up that we're going to receive a blessing from sin, only to have our hopes dashed after having fallen for it. They are cursed.

I don't believe any of them want to be seen – either the holy or the unholy. The evil ones are criminals who don't want to get caught. When the holy ones appear to men, men are apt to fall down and worship them. Then they

---

33 Charles Henry Ross. Public Domain.
34 Genesis 28:10-12, 32:1-2, Numbers 22:31, Joshua 5:13-6:5, 2 Kings 2:11, 6:17, Luke 2:9-15, Hebrews 13:2, et.al.

have to tell them to get up quickly: "Worship God alone[35]." They can probably get a lot more done without having to constantly stop and correct us.

I don't believe Jesus wants us to see them either. He ended plenty of teachings with, "*He who has ears to hear, let him hear[36].*" But He never punctuated them with, "*He who has eyes to see, let him see.*"

Imagine what would have happened if He had: suddenly everyone would be able to see all of the spiritual creatures surrounding them as they are. Everyone would suddenly be paralyzed with both awe and terror simultaneously.

Diapers of all ages would be filled.

A similar vision is eloquently depicted by C.S. Lewis in his work, "The Weight of Glory:"

> "*[T]he dullest and most uninteresting person you can talk to may one day be a creature which, if you saw it now, you would be strongly tempted to worship, or else a horror and a corruption such as you now meet, if at all, only in a nightmare.*"

Casting ourselves as the man born blind in John Chapter 9, heading into territories unknown, it is necessary for us to have a guide. Hence the necessity to be led by the Spirit.

> Romans 8:
> 14 *For as many as are led by the Spirit of God, they are the sons of God.*

> Galatians 5:
> 18 *But if ye be led of the Spirit, ye are not under the law.*

We don't need to see the cherubim and gargoyles surrounding us. We only need to submit to Jesus, and trust Him to lead us by His Holy Spirit[37]. Since we cannot see, we need ears to hear His voice.

---

35 Revelation 19:10, 22:8
36 Matthew 11:15, 13:9, 13:43, Mark 4:9, Luke 8:8, 14:35
37 This chapter constitutes the original inspiration for this book. The rest developed as I was researching the scripture references.

6. Shepherd

John Chapter 9 ended with Jesus speaking to the Pharisees:

> John 9:
> 39 *And Jesus said, For judgment I am come into this world, that they which see not might see; and that they which see might be made blind.*
> 40 *And [some] of the Pharisees which were with him heard these words, and said unto him, Are we blind also?*
> 41 *Jesus said unto them, If ye were blind, ye should have no sin: but now ye say, We see; therefore your sin remaineth.*
>
> John 10:
> 1 *Verily, verily, I say unto you, He that entereth not by the door into the sheepfold, but climbeth up some other way, the same is a thief and a robber.*
> 2 *But he that entereth in by the door is the shepherd of the sheep.*
> 3 *To him the porter openeth; and the sheep hear his voice: and he calleth his own sheep by name, and leadeth them out.*
> 4 *And when he putteth forth his own sheep, he goeth before them, and the sheep follow him: for they know his voice.*
> 5 *And a stranger will they not follow, but will flee from him: for they know not the voice of strangers.*
> 6 *This parable spake Jesus unto them: but they understood not what things they were which he spake unto them.*

They didn't get it. Jesus was proving to them they were blind. God is referred to as the Shepherd of Israel in many Old Testament passages[38]. Israel's leaders are also referred to as corrupt shepherds: Fleecing instead of feeding God's flock[39]. When Jesus purged the temple of the money changers, He complained that the rulers had made His fathers house, "a den of thieves[40]."

Villages typically had a walled, common sheepfold with one entrance. Local shepherds would all bring their flocks in at the end of the work day to leave them in safety so that they themselves could clock-out. The flocks would mingle. In the morning, they would call their own flocks out[41].

---

[38] Psalm 23:1-6, 80:1, Isaiah 40:11, Jeremiah 31:10
[39] Ezekiel 34:1-5
[40] Matthew 21:13
[41] Chuck Missler taught that the sheepfold was Judaism and that Jesus was telling the Pharisees that He was calling His people out of it.

The porter is the night watchman who keeps the gate. That would be the prophets who opened the door to the Jews to fellowship with God by speaking on His behalf. John the Baptist prepared the way for Jesus[42].

> John 10:
> 7 *Then said Jesus unto them again, Verily, verily, I say unto you, I am the door of the sheep.*
> 8 *All that ever came before me are thieves and robbers: but the sheep did not hear them.*
> 9 *I am the door: by me if any man enter in, he shall be saved, and shall go in and out, and find pasture.*
> 10 *The thief cometh not, but for to steal, and to kill, and to destroy: I am come that they might have life, and that they might have [it] more abundantly.*
> 11 *I am the good shepherd: the good shepherd giveth his life for the sheep.*

Everyone wanted to lead the sheep. The rulers made merchandise of the flock. The invisible minions of the devil wanted to kill and devour the flock. Jesus came to die to save them. Some sheepfolds had no gate. The shepherd would lay in the opening serving as the door of the sheep as well.

> John 10:
> 12 *But he that is an hireling, and not the shepherd, whose own the sheep are not, seeth the wolf coming, and leaveth the sheep, and fleeth: and the wolf catcheth them, and scattereth the sheep.*
> 13 *The hireling fleeth, because he is an hireling, and careth not for the sheep.*
> 14 *I am the good shepherd, and know my [sheep,] and am known of mine.*
> 15 *As the Father knoweth me, even so know I the Father: and I lay down my life for the sheep.*
> 16 *And other sheep I have, which are not of this fold: them also I must bring, and they shall hear my voice; and there shall be one fold, [and] one shepherd.*

The sheep spoken of thus far had been the Jews. The *"other sheep"* are non-Jews who come to saving faith in Jesus. The Bible calls them, "gentiles." If you didn't come from Jewish stock and believe, that's you.

> John 10:
> 17 *Therefore doth my Father love me, because I lay down my life, that I might take it again.*

---

42 John 1:23

18 *No man taketh it from me, but I lay it down of myself. I have power to lay it down, and I have power to take it again. This commandment have I received of my Father.*
19 *There was a division therefore again among the Jews for these sayings.*
20 *And many of them said, He hath a devil, and is mad; why hear ye him?*
21 *Others said, These are not the words of him that hath a devil. Can a devil open the eyes of the blind?*
22 *And it was at Jerusalem the feast of the dedication, and it was winter.*

(This is a break in the time stamp. Up to verse 22, the dialog came about when the man born blind received sight. That was immediately after the woman was caught in the act, which was the day after the Feast of Tabernacles: October. The Feast of Dedication – Hanukkah – was in December.)

John 10:
23 *And Jesus walked in the temple in Solomon's porch.*
24 *Then came the Jews round about him, and said unto him, How long dost thou make us to doubt? If thou be the Christ, tell us plainly.*
25 *Jesus answered them, I told you, and ye believed not: the works that I do in my Father's name, they bear witness of me.*
26 *But ye believe not, because ye are not of my sheep, as I said unto you.*
27 *My sheep hear my voice, and I know them, and they follow me:*

"I told you, and ye believed not." He sounds just like the guy born blind. Chuck Smith pointed out in his commentary that when the shepherd stood at the door and called, all the sheep heard his voice. It's only those with whom it resonated that followed. In modern times everyone has heard the Gospel. With some, it resonates.

John 10:
28 *And I give unto them eternal life; and they shall never perish, neither shall any [man] pluck them out of my hand.*
29 *My Father, which gave [them] me, is greater than all; and no [man] is able to pluck [them] out of my Father's hand.*
30 *I and [my] Father are one.*
31 *Then the Jews took up stones again to stone him.*
32 *Jesus answered them, Many good works have I shewed you from my Father; for which of those works do ye stone me?*

> 33 *The Jews answered him, saying, For a good work we stone thee not; but for blasphemy; and because that thou, being a man, makest thyself God.*
> 34 *Jesus answered them, Is it not written in your law, I said, Ye are gods?*
> 35 *If he called them gods, unto whom the word of God came, and the scripture cannot be broken;*
> 36 *Say ye of him, whom the Father hath sanctified, and sent into the world, Thou blasphemest; because I said, I am the Son of God?*
> 37 *If I do not the works of my Father, believe me not.*
> 38 *But if I do, though ye believe not me, believe the works: that ye may know, and believe, that the Father is in me, and I in him.*
> 39 *Therefore they sought again to take him: but he escaped out of their hand,*
>
> 40 *And went away again beyond Jordan into the place where John at first baptized; and there he abode.*
> 41 *And many resorted unto him, and said, John did no miracle: but all things that John spake of this man were true.*
> 42 *And many believed on him there.*

"I and [my] Father are one." If anyone ever tells you that Jesus never claimed to be God, take them to John 10:30. It's a reference to a prayer the Jews recited everyday called, the "Shema:"

> Deuteronomy 6:
> 4 *Hear, O Israel: The LORD our God is one LORD:*

He was encouraging them all to believe; if not in what He said, then in what He did. The offer of salvation was extended to everyone.

It made them so grateful, they wanted to kill him. Again.

7. Condemned

In John Chapter 11, Jesus didn't square-off with the Jewish officials. That didn't prevent Him from making them angry enough to kill Him though. He made the fatal mistake of raising Lazarus from the dead.

> John 11:
> 47 *Then gathered the chief priests and the Pharisees a council, and said, What do we? for this man doeth many miracles.*
> 48 *If we let him thus alone, all [men] will believe on him: and the Romans shall come and take away both our place and nation.*

Why would the Romans take away their nation? The Romans appointed Herod as the king of Judea. If Jesus was declared Messiah by the people, that would make Him "King of the Jews." That would be tantamount to rebellion against the king appointed by Rome, and thus against Caesar.

So they've moved their justification for killing Him from fealty toward God, to fealty toward Caesar. They made it political.

> John 11;
> 49 *And one of them,[named] Caiaphas, being the high priest that same year, said unto them, Ye know nothing at all,*
> 50 *Nor consider that it is expedient for us, that one man should die for the people, and that the whole nation perish not.*
> 51 *And this spake he not of himself: but being high priest that year, he prophesied that Jesus should die for that nation;*
> 52 *And not for that nation only, but that also he should gather together in one the children of God that were scattered abroad.*

Who's the actual author of this conspiracy? Caiaphas didn't know that he wasn't speaking of himself. The same Holy Spirit that empowered Jesus to raise Lazarus from the dead, was prophesying through Caiaphas, arguing for Jesus to be put to death. Chew on that for a while.

> John 11:
> 53 *Then from that day forth they took counsel together for to put him to death.*
> 54 *Jesus therefore walked no more openly among the Jews; but went thence unto a country near to the wilderness, into a city called Ephraim, and there continued with his disciples.*

In John 10, Jesus said more than once that He came to lay down His life for the sheep. Why couldn't He have simply let them stone Him all those times they wanted to in the last few chapters?

Because He was not condemned to death. He needed to be completely rejected by the Jewish officials to fulfill prophesy that He was the stone the builders rejected[43]. If a dozen of them were to stone Him in anger, the rest of the council could say, "We didn't have anything to do with that."

In order for Him to get them to do that, He had to provoke them. Like all Adam's seed, the Jews were lazy and indecisive. So He had to take on a confrontational posture to prod them to indignation. I thrill at the fearless stance He took in their midst.

G.K. Chesterton eloquently depicted Jesus the Man at the close of his masterpiece, "Orthodoxy:"

> *Solemn supermen and imperial diplomatists are proud of restraining their anger. He never restrained His anger. He flung furniture down the front steps of the Temple, and asked men how they expected to escape the damnation of Hell*[44].

John 10:31 finds Him outnumbered, encircled by furious men grasping for bricks to hurl at Him. Did He run? No. He challenged their righteousness:

John 10:
32 *Jesus answered them, Many good works have I shewed you from my Father; for which of those works do ye stone me?*

In the English translation of "The Confessions of St. Augustine," that I read years ago, one of the things that revulsed Augustine about Christianity prior to his conversion, was that he considered it, "womanish."

That's because religion doesn't present Jesus in His confrontational, aggressive, testosterous pose. The prissy comportment religio-fied men present to the world continues to repel masculine men from the faith today.

The depiction I perceive is that of a meme I once viewed online: a Canadian commando decked-out in all his battle paraphernalia, hunkered-down. The thought-bubble said, *"They've got me surrounded... poor bastards!"*

---

43 Psalm 118:22
44 Chesterton, Gilbert K (1874-1936), Orthodoxy, Ch. IX. "AUTHORITY AND THE ADVENTURER"

In my book, "Legion: Glory Unveiled," I outline how Jesus took this same adversarial – *"C'mon, mess with Me"* – stance against the invisible powers and principalities that haunted and controlled the region.

John Chapter 12 is rich with insightful stuff, but Jesus doesn't square-off with the religious officials. In Chapter 13 He washes the apostles' feet, Judas runs off to betray Him, and He launches into His farewell address to the other 11 apostles.

Chapters 14-17 continue His parting words to His disciples, including His great "High Priestly" prayer that He lifted up for them and for us (the summation of Chapter 17).

In Chapter 18 He is arrested in the garden of Gethsemane, hauled-off to the high priest's house, interrogated and delivered to Pilate: the direct representative of Caesar.

Here He doesn't take the combative stance. That was all intended to bring this about. Now He takes on the stance of the sacrificial Passover Lamb, offering no resistance at all.

In Chapter 19 He is scourged and crucified. Thus endeth the combat scenes in the Gospel of John. What appeared to be defeat was eternal victory[45].

But the scenes in John where Jesus confronts the authorities – calling them liars and thieves, children of the devil, telling them that they will die in their sins, declaring Himself to be God – pale in comparison to the confrontations depicted in the other Gospels – excepting His arrest with no resistance:

> John 18:
> 5 *They answered him, Jesus of Nazareth. Jesus saith unto them, I am he. And Judas also, which betrayed him, stood with them.*
> 6 *As soon then as he had said unto them, I am he, they went backward, and fell to the ground.*

That's the only instance in scripture of what Pentecostals call being, "slain in the spirit." Only He didn't say, *"I am he;"* the word *"he"* was added to the text by translators.

What He said was, *"I AM."*

---

[45] Colossians 2:15

8. Matthew

Celebrating Jesus' confrontational side, let's not forget John the Baptist. His message was, *"Repent ye: for the kingdom of heaven is at hand[46]."* The people of Jerusalem and all Judea resorted to John to be baptized of him[47].

> Matthew 3:
> 7 *But when he saw many of the Pharisees and Sadducees come to his baptism, he said unto them, O generation of vipers, who hath warned you to flee from the wrath to come?*

The Pharisees weren't there to get baptized. They were there to scrutinize his ministry. When Jesus asked them if John's baptism was of heaven or men, they reasoned, *"If we shall say, From heaven; he will say unto us, Why did ye not then believe him[48]?"*

Authorities don't like it when you demonstrate that you're not afraid of them. John spoke to king Herod in the same tone and wound up in prison.

> Matthew 4:
> 12 *Now when Jesus had heard that John was cast into prison, he departed into Galilee;*
> 13 *And leaving Nazareth, he came and dwelt in Capernaum...*
>
> 17 *From that time Jesus began to preach, and to say, Repent: for the kingdom of heaven is at hand.*

The exact same message as John. When John was imprisoned, the authorities thought, "Well that pesky fellow is out of the way," only to hear the same message coming from Jesus. "Oh boy, here we go again."

Even when He is perceived as "Gentle Jesus, meek and mild," while giving the Sermon on the Mount[49], He was audaciously offending the religious officials. Several times He would begin with, *"Ye have heard that it hath been said,"* followed by, *"But I say unto you."*

What they had heard was the law of Moses, taught to them by the scribes. Those were the old rules. When Jesus would say, *"But I say unto you,"* He

---

46 Matthew 3:2
47 Matthew 3:5
48 Matthew 21:25, Luke 20:4
49 Matthew 5:1-7:29

was pitting Himself against them and their teaching, and saying, *"New rules!"*

> Matthew 7:
> 28 *And it came to pass, when Jesus had ended these sayings, the people were astonished at his doctrine:*
> 29 *For he taught them as [one] having authority, and not as the scribes.*

But in so doing, He didn't contradict the law of Moses. His rules were the same only stricter than Moses'. For example:

> Matthew 5:
> 27 *Ye have heard that it was said by them of old time, Thou shalt not commit adultery:*
> 28 *But I say unto you, That whosoever looketh on a woman to lust after her hath committed adultery with her already in his heart.*

And lest He be accused of teaching against the law of Moses:

> Matthew 5:
> 17 *Think not that I am come to destroy the law, or the prophets: I am not come to destroy, but to fulfil.*
> 18 *For verily I say unto you, Till heaven and earth pass, one jot or one tittle shall in no wise pass from the law, till all be fulfilled.*

All was fulfilled at the cross[50]. That's why it's OK to eat bacon now[51].

The Gospel of Matthew is chock full of good stuff, but we don't find Jesus duking-it-out with the officials for quite a few chapters. In chapter 12 He healed a man with a withered hand on the sabbath day, and that's when the Pharisees had a huddle to figure out how to destroy Him[52].

Then they accused Him of casting out devils by the prince of devils. He corrected them with His "house divided" teaching, and warned them against blaspheming the Holy Ghost[53]. I don't think He said that with the matter-of-fact voice inflection of, *"No, that's where you're wrong, you see..."*

---

50 John 19:30
51 Mark 7:15-23
52 Matthew 12:14
53 Matthew 12:22-32

I suspect He said it with a rapid fire succession of words with the tone of, *"That's gotta be the stupidest thing I've ever heard you dimwits!"* He followed it up with:

> Matthew 12:
> 34 *O generation of vipers, how can ye, being evil, speak good things? for out of the abundance of the heart the mouth speaketh.*

The next few chapters are filled with teachings and miracles. Jesus casts the money changers out of the Temple in Chapter 21, but very few sparks flew between He and the rulers. Although it wasn't overly heated, Jesus said things to provoke their wrath.

They arrived while He was teaching in the temple and challenged His authority. He side-stepped it by asking them where John the Baptist got his. Using John's ministry as an example, He told them that tax collectors and whores would enter the Kingdom of Heaven before them[54].

(Matthew was a tax collector.) Then He went back to teaching the crowd.

> Matthew 21:
> 33 *Hear another parable: There was a certain householder, which planted a vineyard, and hedged it round about, and digged a winepress in it, and built a tower, and let it out to husbandmen, and went into a far country:*
> 34 *And when the time of the fruit drew near, he sent his servants to the husbandmen, that they might receive the fruits of it.*
> 35 *And the husbandmen took his servants, and beat one, and killed another, and stoned another.*
> 36 *Again, he sent other servants more than the first: and they did unto them likewise.*
> 37 *But last of all he sent unto them his son, saying, They will reverence my son.*
> 38 *But when the husbandmen saw the son, they said among themselves, This is the heir; come, let us kill him, and let us seize on his inheritance.*
> 39 *And they caught him, and cast [him] out of the vineyard, and slew [him.]*
> 40 *When the lord therefore of the vineyard cometh, what will he do unto those husbandmen?*

---

54 Matthew 21:31

> 41 *They say unto him, He will miserably destroy those wicked men, and will let out [his] vineyard unto other husbandmen, which shall render him the fruits in their seasons.*

They might not have answered so harshly if they realized that they were the wicked men in the parable. They should have: they taught Isaiah.

> Isaiah 5:
> 7 *For the vineyard of the LORD of hosts [is] the house of Israel, and the men of Judah his pleasant plant: and he looked for judgment, but behold oppression; for righteousness, but behold a cry.*

Israel is the vineyard. The servants who were beaten stoned and killed were prophets. Jesus is the son. It's leaders were the husbandmen. Continued:

> Matthew 21:
> 42 *Jesus saith unto them, Did ye never read in the scriptures, The stone which the builders rejected, the same is become the head of the corner: this is the Lord's doing, and it is marvellous in our eyes?*
> 43 *Therefore say I unto you, The kingdom of God shall be taken from you, and given to a nation bringing forth the fruits thereof.*
> 44 *And whosoever shall fall on this stone shall be broken: but on whomsoever it shall fall, it will grind him to powder.*
> 45 *And when the chief priests and Pharisees had heard his parables, they perceived that he spake of them.*
> 46 *But when they sought to lay hands on him, they feared the multitude, because they took him for a prophet.*

As long as Jesus was among the crowd, He was safe from the Pharisees because the crowd loved Him. He told the crowd to obey the Pharisees, but not to act like them. Then He turned His attention to them.

> Matthew 23:
> 13 *But woe unto you, scribes and Pharisees,hypocrites! for ye shut up the kingdom of heaven against men: for ye neither go in [yourselves,] neither suffer ye them that are entering to go in.*
> 14 *Woe unto you, scribes and Pharisees, hypocrites! for ye devour widows' houses, and for a pretence make long prayer: therefore ye shall receive the greater damnation.*
> 15 *Woe unto you, scribes and Pharisees, hypocrites! for ye compass sea and land to make one proselyte, and when he is made, ye make him twofold more the child of hell than yourselves.*

16 *Woe unto you, [ye] blind guides, which say, Whosoever shall swear by the temple, it is nothing; but whosoever shall swear by the gold of the temple, he is a debtor!*
17 *[Ye] fools and blind: for whether is greater, the gold, or the temple that sanctifieth the gold?*

[Jesus explains why their policies are ludicrous.]

23 *Woe unto you, scribes and Pharisees, hypocrites! for ye pay tithe of mint and anise and cummin, and have omitted the weightier [matters] of the law, judgment, mercy, and faith: these ought ye to have done, and not to leave the other undone.*
24 *[Ye] blind guides, which strain at a gnat, and swallow a camel.*
25 *Woe unto you, scribes and Pharisees, hypocrites! for ye make clean the outside of the cup and of the platter, but within they are full of extortion and excess.*
26 *[Thou] blind Pharisee, cleanse first that [which is] within the cup and platter, that the outside of them may be clean also.*
27 *Woe unto you, scribes and Pharisees, hypocrites! for ye are like unto whited sepulchres, which indeed appear beautiful outward, but are within full of dead [men's] bones, and of all uncleanness.*
28 *Even so ye also outwardly appear righteous unto men, but within ye are full of hypocrisy and iniquity.*
29 *Woe unto you, scribes and Pharisees, hypocrites! because ye build the tombs of the prophets, and garnish the sepulchres of the righteous,*
30 *And say, If we had been in the days of our fathers, we would not have been partakers with them in the blood of the prophets.*
31 *Wherefore ye be witnesses unto yourselves, that ye are the children of them which killed the prophets.*
32 *Fill ye up then the measure of your fathers.*
33 *[Ye] serpents, [ye] generation of vipers, how can ye escape the damnation of hell?*

Jesus pronounces 7 woes upon them and called them hypocrites 6 times. He said that they would receive damnation, called them children of hell, blind, fools, serpents and vipers, full of: extortion and excess; uncleanness; hypocrisy and iniquity. He went on to prophesy judgment upon them, and lamented for the desolation of Jerusalem.

His next encounter with them in Matthew is at His arrest and arraignment, when He offered no resistance.

Mission accomplished.

9. Mark

The account in the Gospel of Mark parallels the Gospel of Matthew, albeit in a condensed form. Matthew is 28 chapters long. Luke is 24 chapters. John contains 21 Chapters. Mark is 16 chapters. It's concise, moves fast and removes a lot of incidentals.

He touches on the contention between Jesus and the religious officials, but doesn't emphasize it. The main confrontation is when the Jews demand where He gets His authority from, He asks where John Baptist got his, then tells the parable of the vineyard[55].

But all that stuff in Matthew 23 with the 7 woes and 6 hypocrites is left out.

In fact, it gives more space to one of the scribes in a favorable light. They had just tempted Jesus with the questions, "*Is it lawful to give tribute to Caesar, or not[56]?*" And "*In the resurrection therefore, when they shall rise, whose wife shall she be of them? for the seven had her to wife[57].*"

(In the event that you're not a student of scripture, the answers were, "*Render to Caesar things that are Caesar's, and to God the things that are God's[58],*" and, "*[W]hen they shall rise from the dead, they neither marry, nor are given in marriage[59].*")

Which brings us to:

> Mark 12:
> 28 *And one of the scribes came, and having heard them reasoning together, and perceiving that he had answered them well, asked him, Which is the first commandment of all?*
> 29 *And Jesus answered him, The first of all the commandments [is,] Hear, O Israel; The Lord our God is one Lord:*
> 30 *And thou shalt love the Lord thy God with all thy heart, and with all thy soul, and with all thy mind, and with all thy strength: this is the first commandment.*
> 31 *And the second [is] like, [namely] this, Thou shalt love thy neighbour as thyself. There is none other commandment greater than these.*

---

55 Mark 11:27-12:12
56 Mark 12:14
57 Mark 12:23
58 Mark 12:17
59 Mark 12:25

> 32 *And the scribe said unto him, Well, Master, thou hast said the truth: for there is one God; and there is none other but he:*
> 33 *And to love him with all the heart, and with all the understanding, and with all the soul, and with all the strength, and to love [his] neighbour as himself, is more than all whole burnt offerings and sacrifices.*
> 34 *And when Jesus saw that he answered discreetly, he said unto him, Thou art not far from the kingdom of God. And no man after that durst ask him [any question.*

That was probably a bad career move for the scribe to agree with the Guy all his bosses were trying to frame. But to be canonized in scripture for eternity as one of the good guys is not a bad trade-off long-term.

Jesus knew the heart of every individual He came into contact with. Even though this guy was on the opposing team, Jesus didn't take an adversarial stance with Him like He did with his peers.

As in Matthew, the next interaction Jesus had with the religious officials was after His arrest, where He offered no resistance. But I'd like to return to the good scribe cited above. In a parallel passage:

> Matthew 22:
> 37 *Jesus said unto him, Thou shalt love the Lord thy God with all thy heart, and with all thy soul, and with all thy mind.*
> 38 *This is the first and great commandment.*
> 39 *And the second [is] like unto it, Thou shalt love thy neighbour as thyself.*
> 40 *On these two commandments hang all the law and the prophets.*

"The Law and the Prophets," is another term for the Old Testament: the Word of God. Jesus is the Word of God made flesh[60]. Your relationship with God is vertical. Your relationship with thy neighbour is horizontal. Those 2 axes form a cross. Jesus hung on a cross.

> *"On these two commandments hang all the law and the prophets."*

I consider that to be one of the most picturesque and poetic teachings in scripture.

---

60   John 1:14

10. Luke

Luke didn't accompany Jesus during His ministry. He was a traveling companion of the Apostle Paul and a physician. He was a scholar, as Paul was (There is speculation based on literary style that he and the 1st century historian Plutarch are one and the same). His gospel opens:

> Luke 1:
> 1 *Forasmuch as many have taken in hand to set forth in order a declaration of those things which are most surely believed among us,*
> 2 *Even as they delivered them unto us, which from the beginning were eyewitnesses, and ministers of the word;*
> 3 *It seemed good to me also, having had perfect understanding of all things from the very first, to write unto thee in order, most excellent Theophilus,*

The "Acts of the Apostles," was also penned by Luke. It opens with:

> Acts 1:
> 1 *The former treatise have I made, O Theophilus, of all that Jesus began both to do and teach,*

Both Luke 1:3 and Acts 1:1 address these treatises to the most excellent "Theophilus." He must have been pretty important. Who is this guy? History doesn't tell us for sure.

The New Testament was written in Greek. Americans read it in English. The English language has one word for love: "Love." You can love pizza, bowling, your spouse, trombone music, your dog – same word.

Greek has several words for love, based on the context: "Eros" (Ἔρως) is sensual: "erotic." "Ludus" (Ερωτοτροπία) is infatuation. "Phileo" (φιλέω) is brotherly-love. "Storge" (στοργή) is motherly-love, "philautia" (φιλαυτία) is self-love, "Agápe" (ἀγάπη) is whole-hearted, self-sacrificial love.

If you believe in many gods, you're "pantheistic." If you believe in one god, you're "monotheistic." If you don't believe in any gods, you're "atheistic." the suffix: "theistic," comes from the Greek root, "theos" (θεός): "god."

If you take the Greek root for god: "Theos," and add the Greek root for brotherly love, "Phileo," you get Theos-Phileo: friend of God. The letters

Luke wrote to "Theophilus[61]" (Θεόφιλος) were to anyone who loves God. If you love God, then Luke wrote these letters to you.

Now Paul himself declared that he was too young to have followed Christ's earthly ministry:

> 1 Corinthians 15:
> 8 *And last of all he was seen of me also, as of one born out of due time.*

Nevertheless, Paul met and mingled with the apostles who knew Christ. That would suggest that Luke, his traveling companion also met and mingled with them. So when he states in:

> Luke 1:
> 2 *Even as they delivered them unto us, which from the beginning were eyewitnesses, and ministers of the word;*

This suggests that Luke compiled his history of events from "eyewitness" testimonies that were *"delivered"* unto him.

For example, only Luke's gospel gives a detailed account of the events surrounding Christ's birth. Matthew, Mark and John don't because they weren't there. Well, neither was Luke. So where did he get this scoop?

He interviewed Jesus' mom. After the manger scene Luke writes, *"But Mary kept all these things, and pondered [them] in her heart[62]."* The only story in the gospels from Jesus' childhood is that He was left behind in Jerusalem at age 12 and his parents found Him reasoning with the doctors. Then Luke tells us, *"but his mother kept all these sayings in her heart[63]."*

> Luke 2:
> 43 *And when they had fulfilled the days, as they returned, the child Jesus tarried behind in Jerusalem; and Joseph and his mother knew not of it.*
> 44 *But they, supposing him to have been in the company, went a day's journey; and they sought him among their kinsfolk and acquaintance.*
> 45 *And when they found him not, they turned back again to Jerusalem, seeking him.*

---

61 Strong's Comprehensive Concordance G2321
62 Luke 2:19
63 Luke 2:51

> 46 *And it came to pass, that after three days they found him in the temple, sitting in the midst of the doctors, both hearing them, and asking them questions.*
> 47 *And all that heard him were astonished at his understanding and answers.*
> 48 *And when they saw him, they were amazed: and his mother said unto him, Son, why hast thou thus dealt with us? behold, thy father and I have sought thee sorrowing.*
> 49 *And he said unto them, How is it that ye sought me? wist ye not that I must be about my Father's business?*
> 50 *And they understood not the saying which he spake unto them.*
> 51 *And he went down with them, and came to Nazareth, and was subject unto them: but his mother kept all these sayings in her heart.*
> 52 *And Jesus increased in wisdom and stature, and in favour with God and man.*

That was Jesus' first confrontation with those who would have Him killed.

The "doctors" Jesus reasoned with were doctors of theology. They liked Him when He was 12. When He sparred with them later, only 18-21 years had elapsed. It's possible that some of the same men who reasoned with Him at age 12 were present during the fireworks and remembered Him. I remember minute details of things that transpired at my workplace 20 years ago.

Guaranteed, Jesus remembered each of them.

11. Simmer to Boil

In Luke 3, John baptizes Jesus and His geneology is taken all the way back to Adam. In 4, He was tempted in the wilderness 40 days, then returned home to Nazareth and began His ministry. He escaped an angry crowd who wanted to stone Him, by, again, passing through the midst of them[64].

He incited the riot by claiming to fulfill Isaiah's prophesy of the coming of the Messiah[65].

Luke 5 has Jesus teaching and performing miracles in Capernaum and recruiting the fisherman apostles. He miffed the Pharisees when He healed by forgiving sins, and for hanging-out with sinners. Now He's under scrutiny.

In Luke 6 He healed on the sabbath and the Pharisees were filled with madness[66]. He ordained the 12 apostles, healed many, and taught on the mount. He pronounced blessings on the poor and hungry, and woes upon the rich, full and influential.

In Luke 7 Jesus heals the centurion's servant remotely, then raises the son of a widow from the dead in Nain. He magnifies the office of John the Baptist (which was a shot at the Pharisees in the audience because they didn't submit to John's Baptism).

In that same discourse, Jesus continues to tweak Modern Pharisees of today:

> Luke 7:
> 31 *And the Lord said, Whereunto then shall I liken the men of this generation? and to what are they like?*
> 32 *They are like unto children sitting in the marketplace, and calling one to another, and saying, We have piped unto you, and ye have not danced; we have mourned to you, and ye have not wept.*

Remember how Jesus said in John 10 how His sheep hear His voice and the voice of another they will not follow[67]? "[T]*he men of this generation"* He spoke of above, are the leaders: hypocrites. When they would say, *"Dance,"* Jesus' sheep wouldn't comply. The voice of another they will not follow.

> Luke 7:

---

64 Luke 4:30
65 Isaiah 61:1-2
66 Luke 6:11
67 John 10:3-5

> 33 *For John the Baptist came neither eating bread nor drinking wine; and ye say, He hath a devil.*
> 34 *The Son of man is come eating and drinking; and ye say, Behold a gluttonous man, and a winebibber, a friend of publicans and sinners!*

Here's where you can emulate the Savior by making modern-day Pharisees' heads explode: Tell them that Jesus drank. I've witnessed it first hand (the explosion was emotional, not physical).

I guess it's time to do it again. I wasn't going to camp out here, but it is important for a few reasons: 1. It's true; 2. Religionists brow-beat those who imbibe into believing they are excluded from fellowship with God; 3. That's not true; 4. God loves drinkers; 5. Christ died to save them.

The purpose of teaching the truth that Jesus drank alcohol is not to persuade believers to drink. It's to persuade drinkers that they're acceptable to God as they are, with their beer in hand.

The sin is being a drunkard. You can drink without being a slave to it.

One of my closest friends was a Lutheran pastor. Lutherans drink like Catholics. It's tough, but they can keep up. He pointed out that the same churches that preach against drinking, hold carry-in banquets where morbidly obese people gorge themselves, and they utter not a peep.

The sin of being a drunkard falls under the heading of gluttony. Notice in our passage from Luke that the religionists accused Jesus of both in verse 34. In the previous verse, the act of drinking was specifically associated with "wine." You have to torture the text to make it say otherwise.

Most people who attempt to justify drinking bring up Jesus turning water into wine at the marriage in Cana[68]. Teetotalers will shake their head and tell you that it was grape juice.

You have to drink the Kool-Ade to believe that. It is obviously alcoholic by the reaction of the master of the feast. Why would they accuse Jesus of being a drunkard for drinking Kool-Ade? You have to be one of the blind believers of anything that churchies are ever accused of being to accept that claim.

---

[68] John 2:9

There are two words in the original Greek, translated "wine" in the Bible: 'Oinos" (οἶνος)[69], and "Gleukos" (γλεῦκος)[70]. Oinos is fermented alcoholic wine. Gleukos – from which we get "glucose" (sugar) is grape juice.

"Gleukos" appears only one time in the original manuscripts, translated into English as, "new wine[71]." Those who began speaking in tongues on the Day of Pentecost caused a spectacle, and mockers accused them of having too much grape juice with their breakfast (It was 9 a.m.[72]).

My Lutheran buddy said that whenever someone tells you that "wine" in the Bible is grape juice, ask them if they mixed it from instant powder or frozen concentrate. Because before refrigeration, it was impossible to store grape juice without it fermenting.

When Jesus taught in parables about new wine causing old wine skins to burst[73], it was because fermentation produces 2 things: alcohol and carbon dioxide. People who make their own wine at home monitor the fermentation by putting a balloon over the mouth of the bottle, rather than corking it.

Jesus' teaching make absolutely no sense if He were referring to grape juice.

At the risk of belaboring the point, I want to drive a stake through the heart of a false doctrine. Paul called false teaching "doctrines of devils[74]."

Teetotalers will concede that it's OK to drink wine for medicinal purposes, because Paul admonished Timothy to drink wine instead of water to treat his stomach problems[75]. So medicinal use is holy and just.

> Psalm 104:
> 14 *He* [God] *causeth the grass to grow for the cattle, and herb for the service of man: that he may bring forth food out of the earth;*
> 15 *And wine that maketh glad the heart of man, and oil to make his face to shine, and bread which strengtheneth man's heart.*

God created specific things for specific purposes. According to the psalmist, He created some herbs specifically to make wine to gladden the heart.

---

69 Strong's Comprehensive Concordance G3631
70 Strong's G1098
71 Acts 2:13
72 Acts 2:15
73 Mark 2:22
74 1 Timothy 4:1-5
75 1 Timothy 5:23

> Judges 9:
> 13 *And the vine said unto them, Should I leave my wine, which cheereth God and man, and go to be promoted over the trees?*

Apparently it makes God happy too. Jesus drank.

> Proverbs 17:
> 22 *A merry heart doeth good like a medicine: but a broken spirit drieth the bones.*

So if you catch someone drinking alcohol to make their heart merry (which, per Psalm 104, is it's divinely intended purpose), then according to Proverbs 17, that's medicinal use of God's gift.

> Ecclesiastes 3:
> 13 *And also that every man should eat and drink, and enjoy the good of all his labour, it is the gift of God.*

> Ecclesiastes 9:
> 7 *Go thy way, eat thy bread with joy, and drink thy wine with a merry heart; for God now accepteth thy works.*

God is not anti-fun.

Religionists are. That being said, God is anti-stupid and anti-evil. When people over-use alcohol to conjure a spirit of stupidity, evil follows. That's partially why it's a sin to be a drunkard.

> Proverbs 20:
> 1 *Wine is a mocker, strong drink is raging: and whosoever is deceived thereby is not wise.*

> Proverbs 23:
> 29 *Who hath woe? who hath sorrow? who hath contentions? who hath babbling? who hath wounds without cause? who hath redness of eyes?*
> 30 *They that tarry long at the wine; they that go to seek mixed wine.*
> 31 *Look not thou upon the wine when it is red, when it giveth his colour in the cup, when it moveth itself aright.*
> 32 *At the last it biteth like a serpent, and stingeth like an adder.*

33 *Thine eyes shall behold strange women, and thine heart shall utter perverse things.*

34 *Yea, thou shalt be as he that lieth down in the midst of the sea, or as he that lieth upon the top of a mast.*

35 *They have stricken me, shalt thou say, and I was not sick; they have beaten me, and I felt it not: when shall I awake? I will seek it yet again.*

(I lost track of how many times I've proven those verses years ago.)

Thus endeth the digression into liberty with alcohol.

Back to the Gospel of Luke: The remainder of Chapter 7 Has Jesus dining at a Pharisee's house and a woman washing His feet with her tears, and drying them with her hair. The Pharisee thinks to himself that Jesus isn't a prophet or He would know what manner of sinner this woman was.

Then Jesus answered his thoughts as though they were spoken aloud, depicting her in favorable light as opposed to the Pharisee.

12. Boil

In Luke 8, Jesus casts a legion of demons into a herd of swine, heals a woman from an issue of blood, and raises Jairus' daughter from the dead.

In Chapter 9 Jesus sent the 12 on a preaching tour, empowering them to cast out demons and heal. He fed a crowd of over 5000 with 5 loaves of bread and 2 fish. He was transfigured before Peter, James and John, and cast devils out of a boy at the base of the mountain.

In Chapter 10 Jesus sent an additional 70 disciples on a preaching tour. They returned excited about casting out demons. Jesus taught the parable of the Good Samaritan and hung out with Martha and Mary.

In Chapter 11 He spent the day teaching and casting out devils (not by the power of Beelzebub).

> Luke 11:
> 37 *And as he spake, a certain Pharisee besought him to dine with him: and he went in, and sat down to meat.*
> 38 *And when the Pharisee saw it, he marvelled that he had not first washed before dinner.*

That was an intentional faux pas. Hand-washing before a meal wasn't for sanitary purposes: it was a religious ritual that the officials had added to the Laws that Moses had commanded. Jesus was well aware of the custom: the water pots in John Chapter 2 when He changed the water to wine were present for that purpose. Jesus knew the rule. He broke it to get a rise.

> Luke 11:
> 39 *And the Lord said unto him, Now do ye Pharisees make clean the outside of the cup and the platter; but your inward part is full of ravening and wickedness.*
> 40 *Ye fools, did not he that made that which is without make that which is within also?*
> 41 *But rather give alms of such things as ye have; and, behold, all things are clean unto you.*
> 42 *But woe unto you, Pharisees! for ye tithe mint and rue and all manner of herbs, and pass over judgment and the love of God: these ought ye to have done, and not to leave the other undone.*
> 43 *Woe unto you, Pharisees! for ye love the uppermost seats in the synagogues, and greetings in the markets.*

> 44 *Woe unto you, scribes and Pharisees, hypocrites! for ye are as graves which appear not, and the men that walk over them are not aware of them.*

Now the purpose of the hand washing rite was to ensure that they didn't eat their kosher food with defiled hands. Nothing was more defiled than a dead body or grave. Whereas they were accusing Him of being outwardly defiled, Jesus declared that they were defiled on the inside.

> Luke 11:
> 45 *Then answered one of the lawyers, and said unto him, Master, thus saying thou reproachest us also.*
> 46 *And he said, Woe unto you also, ye lawyers! for ye lade men with burdens grievous to be borne, and ye yourselves touch not the burdens with one of your fingers.*
> 47 *Woe unto you! for ye build the sepulchres of the prophets, and your fathers killed them.*
> 48 *Truly ye bear witness that ye allow the deeds of your fathers: for they indeed killed them, and ye build their sepulchres.*
> 49 *Therefore also said the wisdom of God, I will send them prophets and apostles, and some of them they shall slay and persecute:*
> 50 *That the blood of all the prophets, which was shed from the foundation of the world, may be required of this generation;*
> 51 *From the blood of Abel unto the blood of Zacharias, which perished between the altar and the temple: verily I say unto you, It shall be required of this generation.*

"Woe unto you too!" Gentle Jesus, meek and mild. It is from this passage that we get the phrase, "Won't lift a finger."

When Pilate washed his hands of Jesus' blood, the Jews replied, "*His blood [be] on us, and on our children*[76]." But when the apostles began preaching and performing miracles, the same council of leaders complained that they intended to bring Jesus' upon them[77]. Short memories they must have had.

> Luke 11;
> 52 *Woe unto you, lawyers! for ye have taken away the key of knowledge: ye entered not in yourselves, and them that were entering in ye hindered.*

---

76   Matthew 27:25
77   Acts 5:28

> 53 *And as he said these things unto them, the scribes and the Pharisees began to urge him vehemently, and to provoke him to speak of many things:*
> 54 *Laying wait for him, and seeking to catch something out of his mouth, that they might accuse him.*

It was an ambush from the beginning. Jesus knew they were laying in wait so He didn't. He initiated contact. That concludes Luke 11.

> Luke 12:
> 1 *In the mean time, when there were gathered together an innumerable multitude of people, insomuch that they trode one upon another, he began to say unto his disciples first of all, Beware ye of the leaven of the Pharisees, which is hypocrisy.*

The Pharisees controlled the narrative of the day. Everyone knew they were corrupt. Everyone knew they were hypocrites. And everyone knew that if you said anything like that, they had the power to ostracize you and destroy your livelihood.

Jesus wasn't afraid to say it. It felt so good for the people to hear Him saying things that everyone knew to be true, the crowd trampled one another trying to get closer and hear it. Picture that.

> Luke 12:
> 2 *For there is nothing covered, that shall not be revealed; neither hid, that shall not be known.*
> 3 *Therefore whatsoever ye have spoken in darkness shall be heard in the light; and that which ye have spoken in the ear in closets shall be proclaimed upon the housetops.*
> 4 *And I say unto you my friends, Be not afraid of them that kill the body, and after that have no more that they can do.*
> 5 *But I will forewarn you whom ye shall fear: Fear him, which after he hath killed hath power to cast into hell; yea, I say unto you, Fear him.*
> 6 *Are not five sparrows sold for two farthings, and not one of them is forgotten before God?*
> 7 *But even the very hairs of your head are all numbered. Fear not therefore: ye are of more value than many sparrows.*

That scene is so awesome: Jesus is surrounded by authority figures who are still sucking wind from screaming at Him; they're mad enough to strangle

Him; He turns to the crowd and says, *"Don't be afraid of them My friends,"* and commences to tell them how much God loves them.

I was sitting in a Denny's restaurant one night, reading this passage and it came to life. It was as if I were present as it was going on. It was so thrilling, it was all I could do to restrain myself from standing on my chair and delivering an impromptu sermon to the other diners at 1:30 a.m..

Everyone knows Psalm 23, *"The LORD is my shepherd:"* This passage reminds me of:

> Psalm 23:
> 5 Thou preparest a table before me in the presence of mine enemies: thou anointest my head with oil; my cup runneth over.

Luke 12 is 59 verses long, and Jesus spends that entire span teaching from the Pharisee's house surrounded by seething enemies. Jesus' cup was running over with the Holy Spirit while the Pharisees were boiling over.

13. Yoke

Luke 13 appears to be a scene change. It opens with Jesus teaching, but it doesn't seem to be a continuation from the dinner chat.

> Luke 13:
> 10 *And he was teaching in one of the synagogues on the sabbath.*
> 11 *And, behold, there was a woman which had a spirit of infirmity eighteen years, and was bowed together, and could in no wise lift up herself.*
> 12 *And when Jesus saw her, he called her to him, and said unto her, Woman, thou art loosed from thine infirmity.*

Jesus used that phraseology intentionally. He was baiting the religionists and it worked.

> 13 *And he laid his hands on her: and immediately she was made straight, and glorified God.*
> 14 *And the ruler of the synagogue answered with indignation, because that Jesus had healed on the sabbath day, and said unto the people, There are six days in which men ought to work: in them therefore come and be healed, and not on the sabbath day.*
> 15 *The Lord then answered him, and said, Thou hypocrite, doth not each one of you on the sabbath loose his ox or his ass from the stall, and lead him away to watering?*
> 16 *And ought not this woman, being a daughter of Abraham, whom Satan hath bound, lo, these eighteen years, be loosed from this bond on the sabbath day?*
> 17 *And when he had said these things, all his adversaries were ashamed: and all the people rejoiced for all the glorious things that were done by him.*

If you really want to tick-off someone who's proud, humiliate them. That intensifies their anger toward you exponentially.

> Luke 13:
> 31 *The same day there came certain of the Pharisees, saying unto him, Get thee out, and depart hence: for Herod will kill thee.*
> 32 *And he said unto them, Go ye, and tell that fox, Behold, I cast out devils, and I do cures to day and to morrow, and the third day I shall be perfected.*

He'd already humiliated the religious officials. Now He's casting epithets at the political ruler as well. Guaranteed those boot-lickers ran straight to Herod and told him what Jesus had said. That closes Luke 13.

> Luke 14:
> 1 *And it came to pass, as he went into the house of one of the chief Pharisees to eat bread on the sabbath day, that they watched him.*
> 2 *And, behold, there was a certain man before him which had the dropsy.*
> 3 *And Jesus answering spake unto the lawyers and Pharisees, saying, Is it lawful to heal on the sabbath day?*
> 4 *And they held their peace. And he took him, and healed him, and let him go;*
> 5 *And answered them, saying, Which of you shall have an ass or an ox fallen into a pit, and will not straightway pull him out on the sabbath day?*
> 6 *And they could not answer him again to these things.*

I had to look up "dropsy." The modern term is "edema:" Tissue swollen by fluid. It reminds me of a cartoon a co-worker kept in his toolbox of a patient sitting on an examination table. The doctor says, "No, it's not water. Apparently you're retaining food."

They had brought the man before Jesus to bait Him. He took the bait. *"Now what are you gonna do?"* There were no more bouts in Luke 14. The remainder of the chapter is Jesus teaching.

Luke 15 opens with the Pharisees criticizing Jesus for socializing with sinners. Most of the remainder of the chapter is the parable of the prodigal son.

There is teaching but no sparring in Luke 16. In Luke 17 He healed 10 lepers and taught about the rapture. In the middle of the chapter:

> Luke 17:
> 20 *And when he was demanded of the Pharisees, when the kingdom of God should come, he answered them and said, The kingdom of God cometh not with observation:*
> 21 *Neither shall they say, Lo here! or, lo there! for, behold, the kingdom of God is within you.*

There are many messianic prophesies in the Old Testament, but the Prophet Daniel put a date/time stamp on His arrival[78]. Students of scripture Knew

---
78   Daniel 9:24-25

that it was time. They were waiting for the arrival of the King of the Jews Who would deliver them from the hands of all their enemies and reign forever.

He did all that, only it was spiritual enemies He vanquished – not the Roman empire[79]. Even His disciples were waiting for some glorious kingdom to magically materialize[80].

Luke 18 finds Jesus teaching and healing on the way to Jerusalem. In Chapter 19 He enters Jerusalem and chases the money changers out of the temple.

> Luke 19:
> 47 *And he taught daily in the temple. But the chief priests and the scribes and the chief of the people sought to destroy him,*
> 48 *And could not find what they might do: for all the people were very attentive to hear him.*

In Chapter 20, the rulers question His authority, He questions John Baptists' authority and tells the parable of God's vineyard discussed in other gospels. In Chapter 21 He tells the boys that not one stone will be left standing in the temple. They ask Him when this will happen and He tells them signs.

> Luke 21:
> 20 *And when ye shall see Jerusalem compassed with armies, then know that the desolation thereof is nigh.*
> 21 *Then let them which are in Judaea flee to the mountains; and let them which are in the midst of it depart out; and let not them that are in the countries enter thereinto.*

(This is not germane to highlighting the confrontational aspect of Jesus' personality, but it's good stuff.)

The Roman army sacked Jerusalem in 70 AD. Jesus was crucified circa 33 AD. According to Chuck Missler, there were no Christians in Jerusalem when it was razed. They had taken Jesus' teaching to heart and fled to Petra, a fortress carved out of rock in Jordan (Search for it. It's impressive).

What He had said that piqued the apostles' curiosity was:;
> Luke 21:

---
79   Colossians 2:15
80   Luke 19:11

> 6 *As for these things which ye behold, the days will come, in the which there shall not be left one stone upon another, that shall not be thrown down.*

Herod's temple was exceedingly magnifical. It took 46 years to build[81]. The Romans did not intend to destroy the Temple, but during the destruction of the city, it caught on fire. Much of it was overlaid with gold. The gold melted during the fire and leeched between the stones. In order to recover the gold, every stone had to be removed, fulfilling Jesus' prophesy.

As long as we're off-track, we may as well continue. Jesus was raised by Joseph, His step-father, who is described in scripture as a carpenter. Jesus is referred to as the "carpenter's Son[82]." In modern parlance, a carpenter is a drunken red neck with a claw hammer and a circular saw.

That's not the depiction in scripture. The word, "carpenter," in the original Greek is, "tekton" (τέκτων)[83], which translates to, "builder." It's the root from which we derive the word, "architect:" master-builder. It not only referred to workers in wood, but also stone masons.

When Jesus was walking through the temple and His disciples were pointing out the fancy stones, it's entirely plausible that He and Joseph had cut some of the very stones used in Herod's temple.

That may have nothing to do with the confrontational aspect of Jesus' nature, but stone-cutters and carpenters are not sissy-boys. If you could have witnessed Jesus squaring-off with the religious officials, He would have cast an intimidating presence. It's they who were the perfumed princes.

> Matthew 11:
> 28 *Come unto me, all ye that labour and are heavy laden, and I will give you rest.*
> 29 *Take my yoke upon you, and learn of me; for I am meek and lowly in heart: and ye shall find rest unto your souls.*
> 30 *For my yoke is easy, and my burden is light.*

I have searched high and low and have not come up with a primary source for a teaching I ran across. Per tradition, Joseph had a carpentry shop in Nazareth. His specialty was custom fitting yokes for oxen. He hung a shingle outside his shop that read, "Our yokes fit perfectly."

---

[81] John 2:20
[82] Matthew 13:55
[83] Strong's Comprehensive Concordance G5045

So, when Jesus made that comment in Matthew 11, He was making a direct reference to Joseph's shop that the locals would have been familiar with.

If you were a disciple of a particular rabbi, say, "Bob," then you were under the yoke of Bob. Taking Jesus' yoke upon you meant being His disciple. The yoke of the Pharisees and Sadducees was grievous.

I have discovered that Jesus' yoke is easy and His burden is light.

Back on track, Luke 22 recounts the last supper, Judas' betrayal and Jesus' arrest. Luke 23 has Jesus examined by Pilate and Herod and crucified. Thus endeth the accounts of Jesus sparring in the Gospels.

14. SuperMan

In the Gospels, Jesus squared-off with the earthly authorities. Three days after they executed Him, He got back up again. In the meantime He squared-off with fallen supernatural authorities.

The Apostle Paul wrote 2 letters to the church at Corinth found in the New Testament. In the first one, he addresses a local heresy that there is no resurrection after death. He destroys the rumor rhetorically, then explains the significance of Jesus rising again:

> 1 Corinthians 15:
> 20 *But now is Christ risen from the dead, and become the firstfruits of them that slept.*
> 21 *For since by man came death, by man came also the resurrection of the dead.*
> 22 *For as in Adam all die, even so in Christ shall all be made alive.*
>
> 54 *So when this corruptible shall have put on incorruption, and this mortal shall have put on immortality, then shall be brought to pass the saying that is written, Death is swallowed up in victory.*
> 55 *O death, where is thy sting? O grave, where is thy victory?*
> 56 *The sting of death is sin; and the strength of sin is the law.*
> 57 *But thanks be to God, which giveth us the victory through our Lord Jesus Christ.*

How does that work: How did God give us the victory through Jesus? Remember that sin is the sting of death. In order for death to have any strength over us, we have to be charged with sin. And the strength of sin is the law.

When the Romans would crucify someone, they would nail the ordinance of charges against them to the cross. Pilate posted, *"JESUS OF NAZARETH THE KING OF THE JEWS,*[84]*"* on His cross.

Jesus is the Word of God made flesh[85]. The law is codified in the Word of God, in what the Jews call the "Torah," and Christians call the "Pentateuch:" the first 5 books of Moses in the Old Testament[86]. When they crucified Jesus, they crucified the law. Sin no longer had any strength.

> Colossians 2:

---
84 John 19:19
85 John 1:1, 14
86 Genesis, Exodus, Leviticus, Numbers & Deuteronomy

> 13 *And you, being dead in your sins and the uncircumcision of your flesh, hath he quickened together with him, having forgiven you all trespasses;*
> 14 *Blotting out the handwriting of ordinances that was against us, which was contrary to us, and took it out of the way, nailing it to his cross;*
> 15 *And having spoiled principalities and powers, he made a shew of them openly, triumphing over them in it.*

The *"handwriting of ordinances that was against us"* was the law of Moses (the *"ministration of death"*[87]). Where no law is, sin is not charged[88]. Jesus took the power of the law out of the way, nailing it to His cross, thus nullifying the sting of death for those who believe on Him.

The fallen supernatural authorities Jesus squared-off with before rising were the *"principalities and powers*[89]*"* He spoiled in Colossians 2:15. Just as He was able to enrage and humiliate the earthly authorities during His ministry, so He made a spectacle of the devil's staff.

That word, *"spoiled,"* apekdyomai in Greek (ἀπεκδύομαι)[90], is rendered *"disarmed,"* in modern translations. It is rendered as, *"put-off"* elsewhere[91]. Underground, Jesus stripped the fallen authorities of all their weapons.

> 1 Corinthians 2:
> 7 *But we speak the wisdom of God in a mystery, even the hidden wisdom, which God ordained before the world unto our glory:*
> 8 *Which none of the princes of this world knew: for had they known it, they would not have crucified the Lord of glory.*

"Princes of this world," is a misleading translation. There are 2 words in Greek that are translated, "world," in English: "kosmos[92]" (κόσμος), or cosmos, and "aion[93]," (αἰών) or "eon" in English. "Cosmos," is the physical world or universe. "Eon," used here, translates to "age." A more accurate translation in 1 Corinthians 2:8 would have been, *"princes of this age."*

If the principalities and powers would have known that pouncing upon Jesus' vulnerability would cause their own defeat they wouldn't have done it.

---

87 2 Corinthians 3:6-7
88 Romans 4:15
89 Ephesians 6:12
90 Strong's G554
91 Colossians 3:9
92 Strong's G2889
93 Strong's Comprehensive Concordance G165

But it was veiled in a mystery from before the world. God planned our salvation before He even created us.

He knew that when He created us, the devil would mess with us. We are not ignorant of the devil's devices[94]. But the devil was ignorant of His.

The picturesque poetry of Colossians 2, *"having spoiled principalities and powers, he made a shew of them openly, triumphing over them,"* is lost on the modern reader; but it was poignant to the contemporary audience.

The Roman Empire would send legions of soldiers marching out to battle in far-off lands. After a victory, they would return in a military procession of triumph, complete with trumpets, drums, banners and pomp. Citizens would line the streets to cheer for their returning heroes.

At the trail end of the procession were prisoners in chains, often naked. The crowd would pelt them with rocks and rotten food. That's what the phrase, "[H]*e made a shew of them openly, triumphing over them,"* actually depicts.

Scripture doesn't provide the screenplay for that scene (We'll probably get to watch the video when we arrive).

> 1 Peter 3:
> 18 *For Christ also hath once suffered for sins, the just for the unjust, that he might bring us to God, being put to death in the flesh, but quickened by the Spirit:*
> 19 *By which also he went and preached unto the spirits in prison;*

Peter says Jesus preached to spirits in prison while He was down under. It doesn't say what He preached to them (theological controversy). It may be that they were the crowd He was parading the captives past.

Or, perhaps the Prophet Isaiah depicted it hundreds of years earlier:

> Isaiah 14:
> 9 *Hell from beneath is moved for thee to meet thee at thy coming: it stirreth up the dead for thee, even all the chief ones of the earth; it hath raised up from their thrones all the kings of the nations.*
> 10 *All they shall speak and say unto thee, Art thou also become weak as we? art thou become like unto us?*
> 11 *Thy pomp is brought down to the grave, and the noise of thy viols: the worm is spread under thee, and the worms cover thee.*

---

94   2 Corinthians 2:11

> 12 *How art thou fallen from heaven, O Lucifer, son of the morning! how art thou cut down to the ground, which didst weaken the nations!*

Either way, Jesus saw the spectacle.

> Luke 10:
> 17 *And the seventy returned again with joy, saying, Lord, even the devils are subject unto us through thy name.*
> 18 *And he said unto them, I beheld Satan as lightning fall from heaven.*
> 19 *Behold, I give unto you power to tread on serpents and scorpions, and over all the power of the enemy: and nothing shall by any means hurt you.*
> 20 *Notwithstanding in this rejoice not, that the spirits are subject unto you; but rather rejoice, because your names are written in heaven.*

So when 1 Corinthians 15:57 said, *"But thanks be to God, which giveth us the victory through our Lord Jesus Christ"* (A.K.A. "SuperMan"), that's how he did it. He punked both the natural and supernatural powers that were.

When God created Adam, He gave him dominion over all creation[95]. When Adam screwed up by submitting to the serpent[96], he ceded that dominion to the devil[97]. After the devil screwed up by using that power to crucify someone who had never committed sin (prerequisite), Jesus told the disciples:

> Matthew 28:
> 18 *And Jesus came and spake unto them, saying, All power is given unto me in heaven and in earth.*

Adam screwed up and gave it to the devil. The devil screwed up and gave it to Jesus. So why isn't everything sunshine and bluebirds? Because Jesus delegated the authority to execute that dominion to His followers.

They're just not very good at it. They don't know that they're super.

---

95 Genesis 1:28
96 Genesis 3:7
97 Romans 6:16

15. Supermen

The last chapter began by examining very truncated text from the "death chapter," 1 Corinthians 15. It only covered stuff germane to Jesus vanquishing the power of death. Here's an expansion:

> 1 Corinthians 15:
> 20 *But now is Christ risen from the dead, and become the firstfruits of them that slept.*
> 21 *For since by man came death, by man came also the resurrection of the dead.*
> 22 *For as in Adam all die, even so in Christ shall all be made alive.*
>
> 35 *But some man will say, How are the dead raised up? and with what body do they come?*
> 36 *Thou fool, that which thou sowest is not quickened, except it die:*
> 37 *And that which thou sowest, thou sowest not that body that shall be, but bare grain, it may chance of wheat, or of some other grain:*
> 38 *But God giveth it a body as it hath pleased him, and to every seed his own body.*
>
> 42 *So also is the resurrection of the dead. It is sown in corruption; it is raised in incorruption:*
> 43 *It is sown in dishonour; it is raised in glory: it is sown in weakness; it is raised in power:*
> 44 *It is sown a natural body; it is raised a spiritual body. There is a natural body, and there is a spiritual body.*
> 45 *And so it is written, The first man Adam was made a living soul; the last Adam was made a quickening spirit.*
> 46 *Howbeit that was not first which is spiritual, but that which is natural; and afterward that which is spiritual.*
> 47 *The first man is of the earth, earthy: the second man is the Lord from heaven.*
> 48 *As is the earthy, such are they also that are earthy: and as is the heavenly, such are they also that are heavenly.*
> 49 *And as we have borne the image of the earthy, we shall also bear the image of the heavenly.*
> 50 *Now this I say, brethren, that flesh and blood cannot inherit the kingdom of God; neither doth corruption inherit incorruption.*
> 51 *Behold, I shew you a mystery; We shall not all sleep, but we shall all be changed,*

> 52 *In a moment, in the twinkling of an eye, at the last trump: for the trumpet shall sound, and the dead shall be raised incorruptible, and we shall be changed.*
> 53 *For this corruptible must put on incorruption, and this mortal must put on immortality.*

Here's a technicality many people miss: You and I were not created by God in His likeness at conception. Adam was created. You and I were procreated in Adam's likeness.

> Genesis 5:
> 1 *This is the book of the generations of Adam. In the day that God created man, in the likeness of God made he him;*
> 2 *Male and female created he them; and blessed them, and called their name Adam, in the day when they were created.*
> 3 *And Adam lived an hundred and thirty years, and begat a son in his own likeness, after his image; and called his name Seth:*

Adam was created by God. You and I were begotten – not created – by Adam's descendants in his likeness, to include the fallen nature that the Likeness of God didn't come equipped with.

Since Jesus wasn't conceived by a man but begotten by God, He didn't have a fallen nature. That's partially why Jesus is referred to as the *"last Adam:"* He and Adam are the only two men ever to live without sin.

The Apostle Peter wrote:

> 1 Peter 1:
> 3 *Blessed be the God and Father of our Lord Jesus Christ, which according to his abundant mercy hath begotten us again unto a lively hope by the resurrection of Jesus Christ from the dead,*
>
> 23 *Being born again, not of corruptible seed, but of incorruptible, by the word of God, which liveth and abideth for ever.*

In Peter's phraseology, salvation through faith in Jesus through the power of God is being begotten by the Father (as Jesus was) and being born again.

Jesus told Nicodemus that unless a man is born again, he cannot see the Kingdom of God[98].

---

98 John 3:3

> John 3:
> 4 *Nicodemus saith unto him, How can a man be born when he is old? can he enter the second time into his mother's womb, and be born?*

When you came into this world, you were procreated in the likeness of the first Adam. When (if) you came to faith in the last Adam – Jesus – receiving Him as Savior, your new self was not procreated, but created.

> 2 Corinthians 5:
> 17 *Therefore if any man be in Christ, he is a new creature: old things are passed away; behold, all things are become new.*

Nicodemus, a scholar and teacher of the law of Moses, couldn't understand what Jesus was saying because the mystery[99] had not yet been revealed that God was going to create a new species: a superhuman race.

The human race is the descendant of the first Adam. God told Adam, "*But of the tree of the knowledge of good and evil, thou shalt not eat of it: for in the day that thou eatest thereof thou shalt surely die[100].*" Adam ate of it.

(Digression: *But Adam lived to be 930-years-old[101]. So, did God tell a fib? Technically, no. A day with the LORD is as 1000 years, and 1000 years as a day[102]. The oldest biblically recorded human was Methuselah: 969. So no human ever lived beyond a day on God's calendar.*)

Humans are 3-part beings: Human spirit, soul and body. On the day that they ate of the forbidden fruit, the human spirit died. When scripture tells us that we were born dead in trespasses and sins[103], it means spiritually dead.

When you become born again – into the race of the Last Adam; the superhuman race – begotten by the Father – you don't receive a human spirit: You receive the Holy Spirit[104]. No longer human, you're superhuman.

You have the Holy Spirit of God resident within you. The human spirit is corruptible. God's Spirit is incorruptible. You can't spiritually die[105].

---

99 1 Peter 1:10-12
100 Genesis 2:17
101 Genesis 5:5
102 Psalm 90:4, 2 Peter 3:8
103 Ephesians 2:1, Colossians 2:13
104 1 Corinthians 3:16, Ephesians 5:18, 2 Timothy 1:14, 1 John 4:13
105 John 3:16

Occasionally, biblical authorities had to deal with obnoxious characters, anointed with the Holy Spirit called, "prophets." So they persecuted and killed them. Once they had to deal with One obnoxious Character filled with the Holy Spirit: Jesus. So they killed Him.

Because they did, now they're confronted with millions of believers who have the Holy Spirit within them. For the first few centuries they persecuted and killed believers. The more they did, the more the obnoxious faith spread.

So they changed tactics: They adopted the faith as the official government religion and took control of it. So believers stopped being obnoxious supermen, becoming docile and subservient. Whew. Glad that's over.

That's why they don't exercise the authority Christ delegated to them over all creation, and don't fulfill their commission to take dominion[106]. They just forgot that they're superhuman. They've been deceived out of it for around 1700 years.

The one orchestrating the deception is the one Jesus disarmed 2000 years ago[107]. They've also forgotten that he's disarmed.

Per the previous chapter, Adam screwed up and handed dominion of creation over to the devil. The devil screwed up and handed it over to Jesus. Jesus delegated the authority to execute that dominion to His followers.

So, many believers believe that when we pray, *"Thy kingdom come, Thy will be done, on Earth as it is in Heaven,"* that means that the church (all believers corporately) is supposed to take over the governments and establish the Kingdom of God on Earth.

That wouldn't work any better than it did when the government took over the church. They are separate entities instituted by God[108] for separate purposes. A cursory glance at the unity and harmony found in an average church will dispel that fantasy. Why are there thousands of denominations?

Because Jesus told the devil that a house divided against itself cannot stand. The devil's house runs like a sewing machine (albeit unarmed). All he had to do was sow discord among the church to divide God's house. It doesn't matter that the devil is disarmed if the church can't stand.

---

[106] Matthew 28:18-20, Mark 16:15-18
[107] John 8:44, 2 John 1:7
[108] Romans 13:3-4

If the church isn't supposed to impose dominion over creation via government authority, how are they supposed to do it? Through prayer.

> Ephesians 6:
> 10 *Finally, my brethren, be strong in the Lord, and in the power of his might.*
> 11 *Put on the whole armour of God, that ye may be able to stand against the wiles of the devil.*
> 12 *For we wrestle not against flesh and blood, but against principalities, against powers, against the rulers of the darkness of this world, against spiritual wickedness in high places.*
> 13 *Wherefore take unto you the whole armour of God, that ye may be able to withstand in the evil day, and having done all, to stand.*
>
> 18 *Praying always with all prayer and supplication in the Spirit, and watching thereunto with all perseverance and supplication for all saints;*

The devil doesn't have weapons, but he does have *"wiles."* He would be wiley even if the church did have unity. As of this writing, it's a cake walk for him. Paul wrote how a church service should be conducted:

> 1 Timothy 2:
> 1 *I exhort therefore, that, first of all, supplications, prayers, intercessions, and giving of thanks, be made for all men;*
> 2 *For kings, and for all that are in authority; that we may lead a quiet and peaceable life in all godliness and honesty.*
> 3 *For this is good and acceptable in the sight of God our Saviour;*
> 4 *Who will have all men to be saved, and to come unto the knowledge of the truth.*
> 5 *For there is one God, and one mediator between God and men, the man Christ Jesus;*

If the church were supposed to overthrow the world's governments, why would Paul (writing by the Holy Spirit) say to pray for *"For kings, and for all that are in authority?"* Why not rather, *"To Arms! Rise Up!"*?

We have access to God. Jesus is our direct Representative before Him. Why would anyone with influence to that much power waste their time trying to influence corrupt Congressmen or Governors? Jesus told Pilate that His kingdom is not of this world.[109]

---

109 John 18:36

If you can Get God to bless your political supplication, i.e.: repeal an amendment to the Constitution; there is no earthly legislature or executive that can stand in the way of your victory.

The invisible powers control the visible powers. The dark side is busy as a beaver trying to destroy civilization. The light side is waiting for believers to do their job by praying and engaging in spiritual warfare.

(The late deliverance minister Derek Prince wrote a book entitled, "Shaping History Through Prayer and Fasting[110]," that spells all that out in detail, with examples. It's still in print. I've never read it, so I haven't plagiarized it here. But I've watched videos of him preaching on the subject.)

If we continue to sign petitions and stage protests on Earth, we're appealing to powers that are largely controlled by the devil; and will continue to be losers.

If we exercise the authority we have been delegated and appeal to the ultimate Power: the Creator of the Universe, we'll be Supermen.

But a Superman divided can't fly.

---

[110] Shaping History through Prayer and Fasting, © 1973 Whitaker House

16. Stealth

On the night of His arrest, Jesus told the boys:

> John 14:
> 12 *Verily, verily, I say unto you, He that believeth on me, the works that I do shall he do also; and greater works than these shall he do; because I go unto my Father.*

Of the things Jesus said that were hard to believe, that one is toward the top of the list. How could anyone do greater works than calming storms, walking on water, raising the dead and giving sight to the blind?

> John 14:
> 16 *And I will pray the Father, and he shall give you another Comforter, that he may abide with you for ever;*
> 17 *Even the Spirit of truth; whom the world cannot receive, because it seeth him not, neither knoweth him: but ye know him; for he dwelleth with you, and shall be in you.*
> 18 *I will not leave you comfortless: I will come to you.*
>
> 23 *Jesus answered and said unto him, If a man love me, he will keep my words: and my Father will love him, and we will come unto him, and make our abode with him.*
> 24 *He that loveth me not keepeth not my sayings: and the word which ye hear is not mine, but the Father's which sent me.*
> 25 *These things have I spoken unto you, being yet present with you.*
> 26 *But the Comforter, which is the Holy Ghost, whom the Father will send in my name, he shall teach you all things, and bring all things to your remembrance, whatsoever I have said unto you.*
> 27 *Peace I leave with you, my peace I give unto you: not as the world giveth, give I unto you. Let not your heart be troubled, neither let it be afraid.*
> 28 *Ye have heard how I said unto you, I go away, and come again unto you. If ye loved me, ye would rejoice, because I said, I go unto the Father: for my Father is greater than I.*
> 29 *And now I have told you before it come to pass, that, when it is come to pass, ye might believe.*
> 30 *Hereafter I will not talk much with you: for the prince of this world cometh, and hath nothing in me.*
> 31 *But that the world may know that I love the Father; and as the Father gave me commandment, even so I do. Arise, let us go hence.*

> John 15:
>
> *26 But when the Comforter is come, whom I will send unto you from the Father, even the Spirit of truth, which proceedeth from the Father, he shall testify of me:*
>
> *27 And ye also shall bear witness, because ye have been with me from the beginning.*
>
> John 16:
>
> *5 But now I go my way to him that sent me; and none of you asketh me, Whither goest thou?*
>
> *6 But because I have said these things unto you, sorrow hath filled your heart.*
>
> *7 Nevertheless I tell you the truth; It is expedient for you that I go away: for if I go not away, the Comforter will not come unto you; but if I depart, I will send him unto you.*
>
> John 16:
>
> *13 Howbeit when he, the Spirit of truth, is come, he will guide you into all truth: for he shall not speak of himself; but whatsoever he shall hear, that shall he speak: and he will shew you things to come.*
>
> *14 He shall glorify me: for he shall receive of mine, and shall shew it unto you.*
>
> *15 All things that the Father hath are mine: therefore said I, that he shall take of mine, and shall shew it unto you.*

So the means to accomplish the same and greater works is that Jesus sends the same Spirit that empowered His works to empower theirs – and ours. All of John 17 is a prayer that Jesus launched on behalf of His disciples, and those that would believe on Him because of their testimony: That's us.

> John 17:
>
> *22 And the glory which thou gavest me I have given them; that they may be one, even as we are one:*
>
> *23 I in them, and thou in me, that they may be made perfect in one; and that the world may know that thou hast sent me, and hast loved them, as thou hast loved me.*

It's worth reading over and over again. The blessings that Jesus promised to the disciples applies to us as well.

After the Gospels comes the book of Acts of the Apostles. It is a record of them living-out what Jesus told them was going to happen: They would receive His Spirit and carry on His ministry.

Paul wrote:

> Galatians 2:
> 20 *I am crucified with Christ: nevertheless I live; yet not I, but Christ liveth in me: and the life which I now live in the flesh I live by the faith of the Son of God, who loved me, and gave himself for me.*

Acts records several instances of the Apostles being as bold as Christ was in the face of their adversaries. But according to Paul, it was actually Christ continuing to square-off with the authorities through them as proxies.

Not only did Jesus have to provoke the Jews into arresting and killing Him, He provoked Judas into betraying Him. He didn't give any of those promises about sending the Comforter and greater works to the boys until He first ran Judas off. None of those promises applied to him.

The last supper discourse is covered in the Gospel of John, chapters 13 through 17. The evening began with Jesus putting off his outer garments and washing the disciples' feet. That is a common act performed by servants or slaves. Then He redressed:

> John 13:
> 12 *So after he had washed their feet, and had taken his garments, and was set down again, he said unto them, Know ye what I have done to you?*
> 13 *Ye call me Master and Lord: and ye say well; for so I am.*
> 14 *If I then, your Lord and Master, have washed your feet; ye also ought to wash one another's feet.*
> 15 *For I have given you an example, that ye should do as I have done to you.*

That pricked Judas' pride. As mentioned in a previous chapter, the Jews were aware according to the writings of the Prophet Daniel that the time had come for the Messiah to arrive. They were waiting for the Kingdom of God to magically manifest itself. They were prepped for the big time.

The boys knew that Jesus was going to reign as King in this glorious kingdom. James and John had the audacity (or their mother did[111]), to ask that they be able to sit on His right and left hand as He reigned[112].

---

111 Matthew 20:20
112 Mark 10:35-37

Judas held the money bag in the entourage. That meant that when the magic kingdom materialized, He was going to be the treasurer for the nation of Israel. He had been dipping into the till and was looking forward to greater wealth[113]. They were all anticipating glory.

Then Jesus said, *"Humble yourselves and wash each others' feet."* That was the breaking point for Judas. That burst his fantasy bubble of glory and riches.

I've been an arrogant jerk before. I repent. But I can almost hear Judas' thoughts in response to the command to foot wash: *"Not me! I'm no slave. This isn't what I signed up for."* No, he signed up for much worse.

Immediately after rejoining them at the table Jesus said that one of them would betray Him. As they questioned who it might be, He told the one next to him that it was he to whom He would hand sop, and gave it to Judas.

> John 13:
> 27 *And after the sop Satan entered into him. Then said Jesus unto him, That thou doest, do quickly.*
> 28 *Now no man at the table knew for what intent he spake this unto him.*
> 29 *For some of them thought, because Judas had the bag, that Jesus had said unto him, Buy those things that we have need of against the feast; or, that he should give something to the poor.*
> 30 *He then having received the sop went immediately out: and it was night.*
> 31 *Therefore, when he was gone out, Jesus said, Now is the Son of man glorified, and God is glorified in him.*

I contend due to the timing and delivery that a primary purpose of the Maundy Thursday foot washing was to provoke the betrayal. He even commanded Satan to do it quickly.

It was a clandestine confrontation. Just like the sermon on the mount, even when He's portraying Himself as gentle Jesus, meek and mild, He's still poking the devil in the ribs and saying, *"Bring it."*

---

113 John 12:6

17. Tough Guys

> John 16:
> 7 *Nevertheless I tell you the truth; It is expedient for you that I go away: for if I go not away, the Comforter will not come unto you; but if I depart, I will send him unto you.*

The previous chapter discussed how Jesus empowered the disciples to do the same and greater works than He by giving them the same Spirit that empowered Him to accomplish His feats.

It's probably a flawed analogy, but in my mind, it's as though Jesus was the earthly container of the Holy Ghost. In order for Jesus to pour out the Spirit upon them the container had to be broken, just like the alabaster box of precious ointment that the woman anointed His head with[114].

In denying himself to be the Messiah, John Baptist told the crowd:

> Matthew 3:
> 11 *I indeed baptize you with water unto repentance: but he that cometh after me is mightier than I, whose shoes I am not worthy to bear: he shall baptize you with the Holy Ghost, and with fire:*

Acts Chapter 2 provides the record of that prophesy coming to pass:

> Acts 2:
> 1 *And when the day of Pentecost was fully come, they were all with one accord in one place.*
> 2 *And suddenly there came a sound from heaven as of a rushing mighty wind, and it filled all the house where they were sitting.*
> 3 *And there appeared unto them cloven tongues like as of fire, and it sat upon each of them.*
> 4 *And they were all filled with the Holy Ghost, and began to speak with other tongues, as the Spirit gave them utterance.*

Previous to this event, scripture shows the disciples cowering in fear of the Jews behind closed doors[115]. During this event, the Apostles went public and converted about 3000 souls to Christ[116]. And then it was on.

---
114 Matthew 26:7, Mark 14:3, Luke 7:37
115 John 20:19
116 Acts 2:41

In the next chapter, Peter heals a lame man which draws a crowd in the temple. So Peter capitalized on the opportunity to preach Christ to them, accidentally converting another 5000 to Christ[117].

So management had Peter and John arrested and called before the council.

> Acts 4:
> 8 *Then Peter, filled with the Holy Ghost, said unto them, Ye rulers of the people, and elders of Israel,*
> 9 *If we this day be examined of the good deed done to the impotent man, by what means he is made whole;*
> 10 *Be it known unto you all, and to all the people of Israel, that by the name of Jesus Christ of Nazareth, whom ye crucified, whom God raised from the dead, even by him doth this man stand here before you whole.*
> 11 *This is the stone which was set at nought of you builders, which is become the head of the corner.*
> 12 *Neither is there salvation in any other: for there is none other name under heaven given among men, whereby we must be saved.*

So much for cowering behind bolted doors.

> Acts 4:
> 13 *Now when they saw the boldness of Peter and John, and perceived that they were unlearned and ignorant men, they marvelled; and they took knowledge of them, that they had been with Jesus.*
> 14 *And beholding the man which was healed standing with them, they could say nothing against it.*
> 15 *But when they had commanded them to go aside out of the council, they conferred among themselves,*
> 16 *Saying, What shall we do to these men? for that indeed a notable miracle hath been done by them is manifest to all them that dwell in Jerusalem; and we cannot deny it.*
> 17 *But that it spread no further among the people, let us straitly threaten them, that they speak henceforth to no man in this name.*
> 18 *And they called them, and commanded them not to speak at all nor teach in the name of Jesus.*
> 19 *But Peter and John answered and said unto them, Whether it be right in the sight of God to hearken unto you more than unto God, judge ye.*
> 20 *For we cannot but speak the things which we have seen and heard.*

---

117 Acts 4:4

21 *So when they had further threatened them, they let them go, finding nothing how they might punish them, because of the people: for all men glorified God for that which was done.*

The primary attribute that stood out about Peter and John to the council was their boldness in verse 13. They weren't accustomed to that. They were the authorities. They were accustomed to people trembling before them.

Since Peter and John were filled with the Spirit of God, was that them being bold, or was that Christ continuing to square-off with the authorities through them? The next chapter finds them preaching and teaching in the temple again, just as they were forbidden to do by the council.

> Acts 5:
> 17 *Then the high priest rose up, and all they that were with him, (which is the sect of the Sadducees,) and were filled with indignation,*
> 18 *And laid their hands on the apostles, and put them in the common prison.*
> 19 *But the angel of the Lord by night opened the prison doors, and brought them forth, and said,*
> 20 *Go, stand and speak in the temple to the people all the words of this life.*
> 21 *And when they heard that, they entered into the temple early in the morning, and taught. But the high priest came, and they that were with him, and called the council together, and all the senate of the children of Israel, and sent to the prison to have them brought.*
> 22 *But when the officers came, and found them not in the prison, they returned, and told,*
> 23 *Saying, The prison truly found we shut with all safety, and the keepers standing without before the doors: but when we had opened, we found no man within.*
> 24 *Now when the high priest and the captain of the temple and the chief priests heard these things, they doubted of them whereunto this would grow.*
> 25 *Then came one and told them, saying, Behold, the men whom ye put in prison are standing in the temple, and teaching the people.*

Imagine the humiliation of the council: All the senate of the nation assembled and said, "Alright. Bring those malefactors before us!" Only to be told, "Yeah, um, we can't. They're not there." That was egg on their faces.

So they arrested them again:

> Acts 5:
> 28 *Saying, Did not we straitly command you that ye should not teach in this name? and, behold, ye have filled Jerusalem with your doctrine, and intend to bring this man's blood upon us.*
> 29 *Then Peter and the other apostles answered and said, We ought to obey God rather than men.*

I don't know when the boldness factor of the faith expired. It certainly seems to be lacking in modern culture.

As the faith grew from 120 on the day of Pentecost to thousands, the Apostles found themselves overwhelmed with attending to the needs of the throng. So they appointed 7 men to take on administrative roles. One of them was Stephen, who wrought great wonders and miracles[118].

This caused Jews of various sects to dispute with Stephen. He whipped them every time[119]. Where does that sort of thinking come from? *"Hmm, here's a guy performing wonders and miracles. I'd better inform him he's not allowed to do that."*

So they suborned liars to accuse him of blasphemy. He was arrested and brought before the council.

> Acts 6:
> 15 *And all that sat in the council, looking stedfastly on him, saw his face as it had been the face of an angel.*

You know what follows is going to be good when the guy's face starts to glow.

Acts Chapter 7 is largely Stephen's soliloquy to the Council. It's mostly a summary of the Old Testament. He had been accused of blasphemy, so his response was reciting his knowledge of the history of the nation.

The first time I read it, that was all Greek to me. I was a heathen. Someone gave me a Bible and said, "Read the New Testament. That's the book of the Christians. The Old Testament is the book of the Jews." So as Stephen was recounting events from the Old Testament, I was oblivious to what he was referring to. And so the glory was lost on me.

---

118 Acts 6:8
119 Acts 6:10

He began at the call of Abraham, then Isaac and Jacob, then the Egyptian captivity, their deliverance at the hand of Moses, into the reigns of David and Solomon. It was all very eloquent and insightful. Then he said:

> Acts 7:
> 51 *Ye stiffnecked and uncircumcised in heart and ears, ye do always resist the Holy Ghost: as your fathers did, so do ye.*
> 52 *Which of the prophets have not your fathers persecuted? and they have slain them which shewed before of the coming of the Just One; of whom ye have been now the betrayers and murderers:*
> 53 *Who have received the law by the disposition of angels, and have not kept it.*
> 54 *When they heard these things, they were cut to the heart, and they gnashed on him with their teeth.*
> 55 *But he, being full of the Holy Ghost, looked up stedfastly into heaven, and saw the glory of God, and Jesus standing on the right hand of God,*
> 56 *And said, Behold, I see the heavens opened, and the Son of man standing on the right hand of God.*

That was more than they could take, so they hurled bricks at him until he gave up the ghost.

Now here's a bit of theological trivia: God Gave Moses the pattern for the tabernacle and the furniture thereof[120]. He gave David the pattern for the temple and the furniture thereof[121]. There were no chairs. That's because the work of the priests on duty is never done.

When Jesus gave up the Ghost on the cross, He said, "It is finished[122]." The work was done[123]. Hebrews 8 tells us that He is our Great High Priest, and that he is seated at the right hand of God[124]. The work is done.

Stephen's testimony before the Sanhedrin brought Jesus to His feet. Jesus drew back the curtain and let Stephen see Him standing there. Stephen received a standing ovation from Jesus. It's the only one in scripture.

> Acts 7:
> 59 *And they stoned Stephen, calling upon God, and saying, Lord Jesus, receive my spirit.*

---

120 Exodus 25:9
121 1 Chronicles 28:18-19
122 John 19:30
123 Hebrews 9:22-28
124 Hebrews 8:1, 10:12, 12:2

> 60 *And he kneeled down, and cried with a loud voice, Lord, lay not this sin to their charge. And when he had said this, he fell asleep.*

You would think that if a man or woman had such an intense presence of the Holy Spirit, that everywhere they went people were healed, the lepers were cleansed, the dead were raised, the deaf heard and the blind received sight; that it would prompt the applause of the masses and the authorities.

And it did prompt the applause of the masses. But the authorities want all adulation and applause directed toward them. When they feel like you're treading on their turf, they retaliate. That's what got John Baptist killed. that's what got Jesus killed. That's why almost all apostles were martyred.

If you've come to saving faith in Jesus, you have the same Holy Spirit that they had resident within you. Before you decide to sell out for Jesus and become a conduit of the Holy Spirit to flow upon others, know that it might get you killed as well.

Stephen didn't flinch while presenting the truth of God to the religionists, even though it got him killed. He knew where his loyalty lied. I left out one significant verse in the account of his martydom:

> Acts 7:
> 58 *And cast him out of the city, and stoned him: and the witnesses laid down their clothes at a young man's feet, whose name was Saul.*

18. Saul

> Acts 8:
> 1 *And Saul was consenting unto his death. And at that time there was a great persecution against the church which was at Jerusalem; and they were all scattered abroad throughout the regions of Judaea and Samaria, except the apostles.*
> 2 *And devout men carried Stephen to his burial, and made great lamentation over him.*
> 3 *As for Saul, he made havock of the church, entering into every house, and haling men and women committed them to prison.*
> 4 *Therefore they that were scattered abroad went every where preaching the word.*

The authorities persecuted the church to stop the spread of the faith and the persecution became the catalyst of the spread. Prior to that, it was a local phenomenon. It wasn't just the temple officials doing the persecution either: King Herod executed the Apostle James[125]. When he saw that it pleased the Jews, he had Peter arrested so that he could kill him too[126].

(But God broke him out of jail[127].)

> Acts 9:
> 1 *And Saul, yet breathing out threatenings and slaughter against the disciples of the Lord, went unto the high priest,*
> 2 *And desired of him letters to Damascus to the synagogues, that if he found any of this way, whether they were men or women, he might bring them bound unto Jerusalem.*

Jesus appeared to Saul on the way to Damascus and gave him a change of heart, and he went on to be the most zealous defender of *"this way."*

After Acts 13:9, Saul is referred to as Paul. The name "Saul" (Σαῦλος[128]) translates to "desired." "Paul," (Παῦλος[129]) means "small." He considered himself the least of the Apostles because he once persecuted the church[130]. Some scholars claim that "Saul" was merely his Jewish name, while "Paul" was his Roman name. There was no change, they were both his name.

---

125 Acts 12:1-2
126 Acts 12:3
127 Acts 12:7-11
128 Strong's Comprehensive Concordance G4569
129 Strong's G3972
130 1 Corinthians 15:9

At the time of the Apostles there was no New Testament. Paul knew the Old Testament inside and out. So when Christ converted him, he was able to begin preaching the Gospel out of the scriptures immediately. That caused the Jews in Damascus to seek to kill him so he escaped.

> Galatians 1:
> 11 *But I certify you, brethren, that the gospel which was preached of me is not after man.*
> 12 *For I neither received it of man, neither was I taught it, but by the revelation of Jesus Christ.*
>
> 17 *Neither went I up to Jerusalem to them which were apostles before me; but I went into Arabia, and returned again unto Damascus.*
> 18 *Then after three years I went up to Jerusalem to see Peter, and abode with him fifteen days.*

There are mysteries that were not revealed since the beginning of the world that Jesus revealed to Paul during those three years, and he revealed them to the world in penning a substantial portion of the New Testament.

Paul had established a church in the city of Corinth. Then he continued in his missionary journeys. Later, critics came to Corinth and impugned his integrity. So in a letter to the Corinthians he laid out his rebuttal:

> 2 Corinthians 11:
> 22 *Are they Hebrews? so am I. Are they Israelites? so am I. Are they the seed of Abraham? so am I.*
> 23 *Are they ministers of Christ? (I speak as a fool) I am more; in labours more abundant, in stripes above measure, in prisons more frequent, in deaths oft.*
> 24 *Of the Jews five times received I forty stripes save one.*
> 25 *Thrice was I beaten with rods, once was I stoned, thrice I suffered shipwreck, a night and a day I have been in the deep;*
> 26 *In journeyings often, in perils of waters, in perils of robbers, in perils by mine own countrymen, in perils by the heathen, in perils in the city, in perils in the wilderness, in perils in the sea, in perils among false brethren;*
> 27 *In weariness and painfulness, in watchings often, in hunger and thirst, in fastings often, in cold and nakedness.*
> 28 *Beside those things that are without, that which cometh upon me daily, the care of all the churches.*
> 29 *Who is weak, and I am not weak? who is offended, and I burn not?*

> 30 *If I must needs glory, I will glory of the things which concern mine infirmities.*
> 31 *The God and Father of our Lord Jesus Christ, which is blessed for evermore, knoweth that I lie not.*
> 32 *In Damascus the governor under Aretas the king kept the city of the Damascenes with a garrison, desirous to apprehend me:*
> 33 *And through a window in a basket was I let down by the wall, and escaped his hands.*

Those were the persecution dues that he'd paid. When he was arrested at Jerusalem, he laid out his religious credentials to the Jews:

> Acts 22:
> 3 *I am verily a man which am a Jew, born in Tarsus, a city in Cilicia, yet brought up in this city at the feet of Gamaliel, and taught according to the perfect manner of the law of the fathers, and was zealous toward God, as ye all are this day.*
> 4 *And I persecuted this way unto the death, binding and delivering into prisons both men and women.*
> 5 *As also the high priest doth bear me witness, and all the estate of the elders: from whom also I received letters unto the brethren, and went to Damascus, to bring them which were there bound unto Jerusalem, for to be punished.*

Paul had a routine while on his missionary journeys: He'd come to a town and teach in the synagogue. When he would present Jesus as the Messiah, Jews would argue with him and he would reason out of the scriptures. Eventually the synagogues would reject his gospel and he would take the message to the heathen.

He usually started a riot everywhere he went. If it wasn't prompted by the Jewish officials[131], it was prompted by the silversmiths because people weren't buying their pagan idols anymore[132].

I heard one preacher comment that we need more riots.

When he was taken before the council to be tried in Jerusalem he did it again:

> Acts 23:

---
131 Acts 17:5-9
132 Acts 19:21-41

> 1 *And Paul, earnestly beholding the council, said, Men and brethren, I have lived in all good conscience before God until this day.*
> 2 *And the high priest Ananias commanded them that stood by him to smite him on the mouth.*
> 3 *Then said Paul unto him, God shall smite thee, thou whited wall: for sittest thou to judge me after the law, and commandest me to be smitten contrary to the law?*
> 4 *And they that stood by said, Revilest thou God's high priest?*
> 5 *Then said Paul, I wist not, brethren, that he was the high priest: for it is written, Thou shalt not speak evil of the ruler of thy people.*
> 6 *But when Paul perceived that the one part were Sadducees, and the other Pharisees, he cried out in the council, Men and brethren, I am a Pharisee, the son of a Pharisee: of the hope and resurrection of the dead I am called in question.*
> 7 *And when he had so said, there arose a dissension between the Pharisees and the Sadducees: and the multitude was divided.*
> 8 *For the Sadducees say that there is no resurrection, neither angel, nor spirit: but the Pharisees confess both.*
> 9 *And there arose a great cry: and the scribes that were of the Pharisees' part arose, and strove, saying, We find no evil in this man: but if a spirit or an angel hath spoken to him, let us not fight against God.*
> 10 *And when there arose a great dissension, the chief captain, fearing lest Paul should have been pulled in pieces of them, commanded the soldiers to go down, and to take him by force from among them, and to bring him into the castle.*

I thought you were supposed to turn the other cheek, not blurt out, "*God shall smite thee, thou whited wall!*" And he intentionally threw them into a tizzy when he cried, "*I am a Pharisee, the son of a Pharisee: of the hope and resurrection of the dead I am called in question!*"

Even though Paul was the one in fetters, he took command of the narrative and dictated the outcome. As to his cheek, his response to the smite was very similar to Jesus' reaction after having been smitten under identical circumstances. If he was out of line for reacting that way, Jesus was out of line:

> John 18:
> 19 *The high priest then asked Jesus of his disciples, and of his doctrine.*

> 20 *Jesus answered him, I spake openly to the world; I ever taught in the synagogue, and in the temple, whither the Jews always resort; and in secret have I said nothing.*
> 21 *Why askest thou me? ask them which heard me, what I have said unto them: behold, they know what I said.*
> 22 *And when he had thus spoken, one of the officers which stood by struck Jesus with the palm of his hand, saying, Answerest thou the high priest so?*
> 23 *Jesus answered him, If I have spoken evil, bear witness of the evil: but if well, why smitest thou me?*

With both the Lord and the Apostle, when the authorities got physical, they got feisty. That's something to bear in mind as we renew our minds[133] in an attempt to be transformed to the image of Christ[134].

---

[133] Romans 12:2
[134] Romans 8:29

19. Return

John baptized Jesus when He was about 30-years-old[135]. Then Jesus was led into the wilderness to be tempted of the devil for 40 days and nights[136]. Then He began His ministry.

> Luke 4:
> 16 *And he came to Nazareth, where he had been brought up: and, as his custom was, he went into the synagogue on the sabbath day, and stood up for to read.*
> 17 *And there was delivered unto him the book of the prophet Esaias. And when he had opened the book, he found the place where it was written,*
> 18 *The Spirit of the Lord is upon me, because he hath anointed me to preach the gospel to the poor; he hath sent me to heal the brokenhearted, to preach deliverance to the captives, and recovering of sight to the blind, to set at liberty them that are bruised,*
> 19 *To preach the acceptable year of the Lord.*
> 20 *And he closed the book, and he gave it again to the minister, and sat down. And the eyes of all them that were in the synagogue were fastened on him.*
> 21 *And he began to say unto them, This day is this scripture fulfilled in your ears.*

The scripture that was fulfilled in their ears was Isaiah 61:1-1/2, because He only quoted half of verse 2:

> Isaiah 61:
> 2 *To proclaim the acceptable year of the LORD, and the day of vengeance of our God; to comfort all that mourn;*

He didn't come to proclaim the day of God's vengeance. That day is coming.

> Psalm 37:
> 12 *The wicked plotteth against the just, and gnasheth upon him with his teeth.*
> 13 *The Lord shall laugh at him: for he seeth that his day is coming.*

Should we eagerly anticipate that day or cringe at the prospect?

---

135 Luke 3:21-23
136 Luke 4:1-2

> 2 Peter 3:
> 10 *But the day of the Lord will come as a thief in the night; in the which the heavens shall pass away with a great noise, and the elements shall melt with fervent heat, the earth also and the works that are therein shall be burned up.*
> 11 *Seeing then that all these things shall be dissolved, what manner of persons ought ye to be in all holy conversation and godliness,*
> 12 *Looking for and hasting unto the coming of the day of God, wherein the heavens being on fire shall be dissolved, and the elements shall melt with fervent heat?*

Peter says that we should be, "*Looking for and hasting unto the coming of the day of God.*" But Amos says:

> Amos 5:
> 18 *Woe unto you that desire the day of the LORD! to what end is it for you? the day of the LORD is darkness, and not light.*
> 19 *As if a man did flee from a lion, and a bear met him; or went into the house, and leaned his hand on the wall, and a serpent bit him.*
> 20 *Shall not the day of the LORD be darkness, and not light? even very dark, and no brightness in it?*

It's not going to be pretty. When Jesus told the boys that there would be an end to all things and they asked him what the signs would be, He laid it out in Matthew 24+25, in which He said:

> Matthew 24:
> 21 *For then shall be great tribulation, such as was not since the beginning of the world to this time, no, nor ever shall be.*

His return will put a stop to escalating wickedness that exceeds anything in history. Consider the implications of that. What tribulations have we seen just in the 20th century?

Under the oppressive hand of communism, socialism, fascism and Nazism, combined with world wars one and two, more people were killed in the 20th century than all the previous centuries of recorded history combined.

> Isaiah 2:
> 10 *Enter into the rock, and hide thee in the dust, for fear of the LORD, and for the glory of his majesty.*

> 11 *The lofty looks of man shall be humbled, and the haughtiness of men shall be bowed down, and the LORD alone shall be exalted in that day.*
>
> Isaiah 13:
> 9 *Behold, the day of the LORD cometh, cruel both with wrath and fierce anger, to lay the land desolate: and he shall destroy the sinners thereof out of it.*
> 10 *For the stars of heaven and the constellations thereof shall not give their light: the sun shall be darkened in his going forth, and the moon shall not cause her light to shine.*

I've intentionally avoided studying end-time prophesies. Too many have done so and become convinced that they knew who the anti-Christ was and what was going to transpire, only to wind up looking like fools. I'm as fallible as they are and look foolish enough already without compounding it with failed predictions. I don't know who Gog or Magog are.

But scripture does provide us with windows wherewith we can view the end:

> Zechariah 14:
> 1 *Behold, the day of the LORD cometh, and thy spoil shall be divided in the midst of thee.*
> 2 *For I will gather all nations against Jerusalem to battle; and the city shall be taken, and the houses rifled, and the women ravished; and half of the city shall go forth into captivity, and the residue of the people shall not be cut off from the city.*
> 3 *Then shall the LORD go forth, and fight against those nations, as when he fought in the day of battle.*
> 4 *And his feet shall stand in that day upon the mount of Olives, which is before Jerusalem on the east, and the mount of Olives shall cleave in the midst thereof toward the east and toward the west, and there shall be a very great valley; and half of the mountain shall remove toward the north, and half of it toward the south.*
> 5 *And ye shall flee to the valley of the mountains; for the valley of the mountains shall reach unto Azal: yea, ye shall flee, like as ye fled from before the earthquake in the days of Uzziah king of Judah: and the LORD my God shall come, and all the saints with thee.*
>
> 9 *And the LORD shall be king over all the earth: in that day shall there be one LORD, and his name one.*

The Lord is going to stand on the mount of Olives and it will split.

> Revelation 6:
> 12 *And I beheld when he had opened the sixth seal, and, lo, there was a great earthquake; and the sun became black as sackcloth of hair, and the moon became as blood;*
> 13 *And the stars of heaven fell unto the earth, even as a fig tree casteth her untimely figs, when she is shaken of a mighty wind.*
> 14 *And the heaven departed as a scroll when it is rolled together; and every mountain and island were moved out of their places.*
> 15 *And the kings of the earth, and the great men, and the rich men, and the chief captains, and the mighty men, and every bondman, and every free man, hid themselves in the dens and in the rocks of the mountains;*
> 16 *And said to the mountains and rocks, Fall on us, and hide us from the face of him that sitteth on the throne, and from the wrath of the Lamb:*
> 17 *For the great day of his wrath is come; and who shall be able to stand?*

> Revelation 19:
> 11 *And I saw heaven opened, and behold a white horse; and he that sat upon him was called Faithful and True, and in righteousness he doth judge and make war.*
> 12 *His eyes were as a flame of fire, and on his head were many crowns; and he had a name written, that no man knew, but he himself.*
> 13 *And he was clothed with a vesture dipped in blood: and his name is called The Word of God.*
> 14 *And the armies which were in heaven followed him upon white horses, clothed in fine linen, white and clean.*
> 15 *And out of his mouth goeth a sharp sword, that with it he should smite the nations: and he shall rule them with a rod of iron: and he treadeth the winepress of the fierceness and wrath of Almighty God.*
> 16 *And he hath on his vesture and on his thigh a name written, KING OF KINGS, AND LORD OF LORDS.*

When Jesus came the first time, He squared-off with the authorities, who were the pawns of powers and principalities, and let them nail Him to a cross. When He comes back the next time, it's not going to be to lie down and take it. It's going to be to give it.

To trample the vintage where the grapes of wrath are stored.

"14 *And the armies which were in heaven followed him upon white horses, clothed in fine linen, white and clean.*"

In excerpt from Zechariah: "*the LORD my God shall come, and all the saints with thee.*"

That's you and I. When He returns to instill justice on earth, those who believe on Him will be His entourage.

Even though the Prophet Amos discouraged us from looking forward to the day of the Lord, the Bible closes with the words:

> Revelation 22:
> 20 *He which testifieth these things saith, Surely I come quickly. Amen. Even so, come, Lord Jesus.*
> 21 *The grace of our Lord Jesus Christ be with you all. Amen.*

Finally:

> Revelation 1:
> 7 *Behold, he cometh with clouds; and every eye shall see him, and they also which pierced him: and all kindreds of the earth shall wail because of him. Even so, Amen.*
> 8 *I am Alpha and Omega, the beginning and the ending, saith the Lord, which is, and which was, and which is to come, the Almighty.*

When He dominated the scribes, Pharisees, Sadducees and lawyers during His earthly ministry, Jesus established Himself as the Alpha-male. All those skirmishes were impressive. But they're nothing compared to what we will witness when He comes back in the clouds, declaring Himself the Alpha and Omega.

When wickedness escalates to a magnitude unprecedented in human history, the Father will unleash Jesus and He will put His foot down. And when He does, He'll crush the head of the serpent.

It will be a display of raw power as never witnessed before. Awe and majesty. So with great trepidation:

> "*Even so, come, Lord Jesus.*"

Return

20. References

Text of the scripture references found in the footnotes.

1. Connecting the Dots

> 1 John 1:
> 1 In the beginning was the Word, and the Word was with God, and the Word was God.
>
> John 1:
> 14 And the Word was made flesh, and dwelt among us, (and we beheld his glory, the glory as of the only begotten of the Father,) full of grace and truth.
>
> 2 John 2:
> 11 This beginning of miracles did Jesus in Cana of Galilee, and manifested forth his glory; and his disciples believed on him.
>
> 3 John 4:
> 10 Jesus answered and said unto her, If thou knewest the gift of God, and who it is that saith to thee, Give me to drink; thou wouldest have asked of him, and he would have given thee living water.
>
> 4 John 4:
> 25 The woman saith unto him, I know that Messias cometh, which is called Christ: when he is come, he will tell us all things.
> 26 Jesus saith unto her, I that speak unto thee am he.
>
> 5 John 5:
> 18 Therefore the Jews sought the more to kill him, because he not only had broken the sabbath, but said also that God was his Father, making himself equal with God.
>
> 6 John 6:
> 66 From that time many of his disciples went back, and walked no more with him.
>
> 7 John 7:
> 25 Then said some of them of Jerusalem, Is not this he, whom they seek to kill?
>
> 8 John 8:
> 6 This they said, tempting him, that they might have to accuse him. But Jesus stooped down, and with his finger wrote on the ground, as though he heard them not.

2. I AM

> 11 Mark 15:
> 34 And at the ninth hour Jesus cried with a loud voice, saying, Eloi, Eloi, lama sabachthani? which is, being interpreted, My God, my God, why hast thou forsaken me?
>
> 15 Exodus 20:
> 7 Thou shalt not take the name of the LORD thy God in vain; for the LORD will not hold him guiltless that taketh his name in vain.
>
> 17 Geneis 22:
> 14 And Abraham called the name of that place Jehovahjireh: as it is said to this day, In the mount of the LORD it shall be seen.
>
> 18 Exodus 3:

14 And God said unto Moses, I AM THAT I AM: and he said, Thus shalt thou say unto the children of Israel, I AM hath sent me unto you.

3. Escalate

20 John 3:
1 There was a man of the Pharisees, named Nicodemus, a ruler of the Jews:
2 The same came to Jesus by night, and said unto him, Rabbi, we know that thou art a teacher come from God: for no man can do these miracles that thou doest, except God be with him.-

John 7:
50 Nicodemus saith unto them, (he that came to Jesus by night, being one of them,)
51 Doth our law judge any man, before it hear him, and know what he doeth?

21 John 19:
38 And after this Joseph of Arimathaea, being a disciple of Jesus, but secretly for fear of the Jews, besought Pilate that he might take away the body of Jesus: and Pilate gave him leave. He came therefore, and took the body of Jesus.

22 Acts 5:
35 And said unto them, Ye men of Israel, take heed to yourselves what ye intend to do as touching these men.
36 For before these days rose up Theudas, boasting himself to be somebody; to whom a number of men, about four hundred, joined themselves: who was slain; and all, as many as obeyed him, were scattered, and brought to nought.
37 After this man rose up Judas of Galilee in the days of the taxing, and drew away much people after him: he also perished; and all, even as many as obeyed him, were dispersed.
38 And now I say unto you, Refrain from these men, and let them alone: for if this counsel or this work be of men, it will come to nought:
39 But if it be of God, ye cannot overthrow it; lest haply ye be found even to fight against God.
40 And to him they agreed: and when they had called the apostles, and beaten them, they commanded that they should not speak in the name of Jesus, and let them go.

23 Job 39:
1 Knowest thou the time when the wild goats of the rock bring forth? or canst thou mark when the hinds do calve?
2 Canst thou number the months that they fulfil? or knowest thou the time when they bring forth?

24 Exodus 3:
14 And God said unto Moses, I AM THAT I AM: and he said, Thus shalt thou say unto the children of Israel, I AM hath sent me unto you.

25 John 4:
12 Art thou greater than our father Jacob, which gave us the well, and drank thereof himself, and his children, and his cattle?

26 Matthew 23:
5 But all their works they do for to be seen of men: they make broad their phylacteries, and enlarge the borders of their garments,
6 And love the uppermost rooms at feasts, and the chief seats in the synagogues,
7 And greetings in the markets, and to be called of men, Rabbi, Rabbi.

27 Exodus 4:
21 And the LORD said unto Moses, When thou goest to return into Egypt, see that thou do all those wonders before Pharaoh, which I have put in thine hand: but I will harden his heart, that he shall not let the people go.

28 John 5:

18 Therefore the Jews sought the more to kill him, because he not only had broken the sabbath, but said also that God was his Father, making himself equal with God.

4. Born Blind

29 Genesis 2:
7 And the LORD God formed man of the dust of the ground, and breathed into his nostrils the breath of life; and man became a living soul.

30 John 1:
3 All things were made by him; and without him was not any thing made that was made.

31 Genesis 1:
3 And God said, Let there be light: and there was light.

32 Genesis 2:
2 And on the seventh day God ended his work which he had made; and he rested on the seventh day from all his work which he had made.

5. Allegory

34 Genesis 28:
10 And Jacob went out from Beersheba, and went toward Haran.
11 And he lighted upon a certain place, and tarried there all night, because the sun was set; and he took of the stones of that place, and put them for his pillows, and lay down in that place to sleep.
12 And he dreamed, and behold a ladder set up on the earth, and the top of it reached to heaven: and behold the angels of God ascending and descending on it.

Genesis 32:
1 And Jacob went on his way, and the angels of God met him.
2 And when Jacob saw them, he said, This is God's host: and he called the name of that place Mahanaim.

Numbers 22:
31 Then the LORD opened the eyes of Balaam, and he saw the angel of the LORD standing in the way, and his sword drawn in his hand: and he bowed down his head, and fell flat on his face.

Joshua 5:
13 And it came to pass, when Joshua was by Jericho, that he lifted up his eyes and looked, and, behold, there stood a man over against him with his sword drawn in his hand: and Joshua went unto him, and said unto him, Art thou for us, or for our adversaries?
14 And he said, Nay; but as captain of the host of the LORD am I now come. And Joshua fell on his face to the earth, and did worship, and said unto him, What saith my lord unto his servant?
15 And the captain of the LORD'S host said unto Joshua, Loose thy shoe from off thy foot; for the place whereon thou standest is holy. And Joshua did so.

Joshua 6:
1 Now Jericho was straitly shut up because of the children of Israel: none went out, and none came in.
2 And the LORD said unto Joshua, See, I have given into thine hand Jericho, and the king thereof, and the mighty men of valour.
3 And ye shall compass the city, all ye men of war, and go round about the city once. Thus shalt thou do six days.
4 And seven priests shall bear before the ark seven trumpets of rams' horns: and the seventh day ye shall compass the city seven times, and the priests shall blow with the trumpets.

References

5 And it shall come to pass, that when they make a long blast with the ram's horn, and when ye hear the sound of the trumpet, all the people shall shout with a great shout; and the wall of the city shall fall down flat, and the people shall ascend up every man straight before him.

2 Kings 2:
11 And it came to pass, as they still went on, and talked, that, behold, there appeared a chariot of fire, and horses of fire, and parted them both asunder; and Elijah went up by a whirlwind into heaven.

2 Kings 6:
17 And Elisha prayed, and said, LORD, I pray thee, open his eyes, that he may see. And the LORD opened the eyes of the young man; and he saw: and, behold, the mountain was full of horses and chariots of fire round about Elisha.

Luke 2:
9 And, lo, the angel of the Lord came upon them, and the glory of the Lord shone round about them: and they were sore afraid.
10 And the angel said unto them, Fear not: for, behold, I bring you good tidings of great joy, which shall be to all people.
11 For unto you is born this day in the city of David a Saviour, which is Christ the Lord.
12 And this shall be a sign unto you; Ye shall find the babe wrapped in swaddling clothes, lying in a manger.
13 And suddenly there was with the angel a multitude of the heavenly host praising God, and saying,
14 Glory to God in the highest, and on earth peace, good will toward men.
15 And it came to pass, as the angels were gone away from them into heaven, the shepherds said one to another, Let us now go even unto Bethlehem, and see this thing which is come to pass, which the Lord hath made known unto us.

Hebrews 13:
2 Be not forgetful to entertain strangers: for thereby some have entertained angels unawares.

35 Revelation 19:
10 And I fell at his feet to worship him. And he said unto me, See thou do it not: I am thy fellowservant, and of thy brethren that have the testimony of Jesus: worship God: for the testimony of Jesus is the spirit of prophecy.

Revelation 22:
8 And I John saw these things, and heard them. And when I had heard and seen, I fell down to worship before the feet of the angel which shewed me these things.

36 Matthew 11:
15 He that hath ears to hear, let him hear.

Matthew 13:
9 He that hath ears to hear, let him hear.

Matthew 13:
43 Then shall the righteous shine forth as the sun in the kingdom of their Father. Who hath ears to hear, let him hear.

Mark 4:
9 And he said unto them, He that hath ears to hear, let him hear.

Luke 8:
8 And other fell on good ground, and sprang up, and bare fruit an hundredfold. And when he had said these things, he cried, He that hath ears to hear, let him hear.

Luke 14:

35 It is neither fit for the land, nor yet for the dunghill; but men cast it out. He that hath ears to hear, let him hear.

6. Shepherd

38 Psalm 23:
1 [[A Psalm of David.]] The LORD is my shepherd; I shall not want.
2 He maketh me to lie down in green pastures: he leadeth me beside the still waters.
3 He restoreth my soul: he leadeth me in the paths of righteousness for his name's sake.
4 Yea, though I walk through the valley of the shadow of death, I will fear no evil: for thou art with me; thy rod and thy staff they comfort me.
5 Thou preparest a table before me in the presence of mine enemies: thou anointest my head with oil; my cup runneth over.
6 Surely goodness and mercy shall follow me all the days of my life: and I will dwell in the house of the LORD for ever.

Psalm 80:
1 [[To the chief Musician upon Shoshannimeduth, A Psalm of Asaph.]] Give ear, O Shepherd of Israel, thou that leadest Joseph like a flock; thou that dwellest between the cherubims, shine forth.

Isaiah 40:
11 He shall feed his flock like a shepherd: he shall gather the lambs with his arm, and carry them in his bosom, and shall gently lead those that are with young.

Jeremiah 31:
10 Hear the word of the LORD, O ye nations, and declare it in the isles afar off, and say, He that scattered Israel will gather him, and keep him, as a shepherd doth his flock.

39 Ezekiel 34:
1 And the word of the LORD came unto me, saying,
2 Son of man, prophesy against the shepherds of Israel, prophesy, and say unto them, Thus saith the Lord GOD unto the shepherds; Woe be to the shepherds of Israel that do feed themselves! should not the shepherds feed the flocks?
3 Ye eat the fat, and ye clothe you with the wool, ye kill them that are fed: but ye feed not the flock.
4 The diseased have ye not strengthened, neither have ye healed that which was sick, neither have ye bound up that which was broken, neither have ye brought again that which was driven away, neither have ye sought that which was lost; but with force and with cruelty have ye ruled them.
5 And they were scattered, because there is no shepherd: and they became meat to all the beasts of the field, when they were scattered.

40 Matthew 21:
13 And said unto them, It is written, My house shall be called the house of prayer; but ye have made it a den of thieves.

42 John 1:
23 He said, I am the voice of one crying in the wilderness, Make straight the way of the Lord, as said the prophet Esaias.

7. Condemned

43 Psalm 118:
22 The stone which the builders refused is become the head stone of the corner.

45 Colossians 2:
15 And having spoiled principalities and powers, he made a shew of them openly, triumphing over them in it.

8. Matthew

46 Matthew 3:
2 And saying, Repent ye: for the kingdom of heaven is at hand.

47 Matthew 3:
5 Then went out to him Jerusalem, and all Judaea, and all the region round about Jordan,

48 Matthew 21:
25 The baptism of John, whence was it? from heaven, or of men? And they reasoned with themselves, saying, If we shall say, From heaven; he will say unto us, Why did ye not then believe him?

Luke 20:
4 The baptism of John, was it from heaven, or of men?

49 Matthew 5:
1 And seeing the multitudes, he went up into a mountain: and when he was set, his disciples came unto him:
2 And he opened his mouth, and taught them, saying,
3 Blessed are the poor in spirit: for theirs is the kingdom of heaven.
4 Blessed are they that mourn: for they shall be comforted.
5 Blessed are the meek: for they shall inherit the earth.
6 Blessed are they which do hunger and thirst after righteousness: for they shall be filled.
7 Blessed are the merciful: for they shall obtain mercy.
8 Blessed are the pure in heart: for they shall see God.
9 Blessed are the peacemakers: for they shall be called the children of God.
10 Blessed are they which are persecuted for righteousness' sake: for theirs is the kingdom of heaven.
11 Blessed are ye, when men shall revile you, and persecute you, and shall say all manner of evil against you falsely, for my sake.
12 Rejoice, and be exceeding glad: for great is your reward in heaven: for so persecuted they the prophets which were before you.
13 Ye are the salt of the earth: but if the salt have lost his savour, wherewith shall it be salted? it is thenceforth good for nothing, but to be cast out, and to be trodden under foot of men.
14 Ye are the light of the world. A city that is set on an hill cannot be hid.
15 Neither do men light a candle, and put it under a bushel, but on a candlestick; and it giveth light unto all that are in the house.
16 Let your light so shine before men, that they may see your good works, and glorify your Father which is in heaven.
17 Think not that I am come to destroy the law, or the prophets: I am not come to destroy, but to fulfil.
18 For verily I say unto you, Till heaven and earth pass, one jot or one tittle shall in no wise pass from the law, till all be fulfilled.
19 Whosoever therefore shall break one of these least commandments, and shall teach men so, he shall be called the least in the kingdom of heaven: but whosoever shall do and teach them, the same shall be called great in the kingdom of heaven.
20 For I say unto you, That except your righteousness shall exceed the righteousness of the scribes and Pharisees, ye shall in no case enter into the kingdom of heaven.
21 Ye have heard that it was said by them of old time, Thou shalt not kill; and whosoever shall kill shall be in danger of the judgment:
22 But I say unto you, That whosoever is angry with his brother without a cause shall be in danger of the judgment: and whosoever shall say to his brother, Raca, shall be in danger of the council: but whosoever shall say, Thou fool, shall be in danger of hell fire.
23 Therefore if thou bring thy gift to the altar, and there rememberest that thy brother hath ought against thee;
24 Leave there thy gift before the altar, and go thy way; first be reconciled to thy brother, and then come and offer thy gift.

25 Agree with thine adversary quickly, whiles thou art in the way with him; lest at any time the adversary deliver thee to the judge, and the judge deliver thee to the officer, and thou be cast into prison.
26 Verily I say unto thee, Thou shalt by no means come out thence, till thou hast paid the uttermost farthing.
27 Ye have heard that it was said by them of old time, Thou shalt not commit adultery:
28 But I say unto you, That whosoever looketh on a woman to lust after her hath committed adultery with her already in his heart.
29 And if thy right eye offend thee, pluck it out, and cast it from thee: for it is profitable for thee that one of thy members should perish, and not that thy whole body should be cast into hell.
30 And if thy right hand offend thee, cut it off, and cast it from thee: for it is profitable for thee that one of thy members should perish, and not that thy whole body should be cast into hell.
31 It hath been said, Whosoever shall put away his wife, let him give her a writing of divorcement:
32 But I say unto you, That whosoever shall put away his wife, saving for the cause of fornication, causeth her to commit adultery: and whosoever shall marry her that is divorced committeth adultery.
33 Again, ye have heard that it hath been said by them of old time, Thou shalt not forswear thyself, but shalt perform unto the Lord thine oaths:
34 But I say unto you, Swear not at all; neither by heaven; for it is God's throne:
35 Nor by the earth; for it is his footstool: neither by Jerusalem; for it is the city of the great King.
36 Neither shalt thou swear by thy head, because thou canst not make one hair white or black.
37 But let your communication be, Yea, yea; Nay, nay: for whatsoever is more than these cometh of evil.
38 Ye have heard that it hath been said, An eye for an eye, and a tooth for a tooth:
39 But I say unto you, That ye resist not evil: but whosoever shall smite thee on thy right cheek, turn to him the other also.
40 And if any man will sue thee at the law, and take away thy coat, let him have thy cloke also.
41 And whosoever shall compel thee to go a mile, go with him twain.
42 Give to him that asketh thee, and from him that would borrow of thee turn not thou away.
43 Ye have heard that it hath been said, Thou shalt love thy neighbour, and hate thine enemy.
44 But I say unto you, Love your enemies, bless them that curse you, do good to them that hate you, and pray for them which despitefully use you, and persecute you;
45 That ye may be the children of your Father which is in heaven: for he maketh his sun to rise on the evil and on the good, and sendeth rain on the just and on the unjust.
46 For if ye love them which love you, what reward have ye? do not even the publicans the same?
47 And if ye salute your brethren only, what do ye more than others? do not even the publicans so?
48 Be ye therefore perfect, even as your Father which is in heaven is perfect.

Matthew 6:
1 Take heed that ye do not your alms before men, to be seen of them: otherwise ye have no reward of your Father which is in heaven.
2 Therefore when thou doest thine alms, do not sound a trumpet before thee, as the hypocrites do in the synagogues and in the streets, that they may have glory of men. Verily I say unto you, They have their reward.
3 But when thou doest alms, let not thy left hand know what thy right hand doeth:
4 That thine alms may be in secret: and thy Father which seeth in secret himself shall reward thee openly.
5 And when thou prayest, thou shalt not be as the hypocrites are: for they love to pray standing in the synagogues and in the corners of the streets, that they may be seen of men. Verily I say unto you, They have their reward.
6 But thou, when thou prayest, enter into thy closet, and when thou hast shut thy door, pray to thy Father which is in secret; and thy Father which seeth in secret shall reward thee openly.
7 But when ye pray, use not vain repetitions, as the heathen do: for they think that they shall be heard for their much speaking.
8 Be not ye therefore like unto them: for your Father knoweth what things ye have need of, before ye ask him.
9 After this manner therefore pray ye: Our Father which art in heaven, Hallowed be thy name.
10 Thy kingdom come. Thy will be done in earth, as it is in heaven.
11 Give us this day our daily bread.
12 And forgive us our debts, as we forgive our debtors.

13 And lead us not into temptation, but deliver us from evil: For thine is the kingdom, and the power, and the glory, for ever. Amen.
14 For if ye forgive men their trespasses, your heavenly Father will also forgive you:
15 But if ye forgive not men their trespasses, neither will your Father forgive your trespasses.
16 Moreover when ye fast, be not, as the hypocrites, of a sad countenance: for they disfigure their faces, that they may appear unto men to fast. Verily I say unto you, They have their reward.
17 But thou, when thou fastest, anoint thine head, and wash thy face;
18 That thou appear not unto men to fast, but unto thy Father which is in secret: and thy Father, which seeth in secret, shall reward thee openly.
19 Lay not up for yourselves treasures upon earth, where moth and rust doth corrupt, and where thieves break through and steal:
20 But lay up for yourselves treasures in heaven, where neither moth nor rust doth corrupt, and where thieves do not break through nor steal:
21 For where your treasure is, there will your heart be also.
22 The light of the body is the eye: if therefore thine eye be single, thy whole body shall be full of light.
23 But if thine eye be evil, thy whole body shall be full of darkness. If therefore the light that is in thee be darkness, how great is that darkness!
24 No man can serve two masters: for either he will hate the one, and love the other; or else he will hold to the one, and despise the other. Ye cannot serve God and mammon.
25 Therefore I say unto you, Take no thought for your life, what ye shall eat, or what ye shall drink; nor yet for your body, what ye shall put on. Is not the life more than meat, and the body than raiment?
26 Behold the fowls of the air: for they sow not, neither do they reap, nor gather into barns; yet your heavenly Father feedeth them. Are ye not much better than they?
27 Which of you by taking thought can add one cubit unto his stature?
28 And why take ye thought for raiment? Consider the lilies of the field, how they grow; they toil not, neither do they spin:
29 And yet I say unto you, That even Solomon in all his glory was not arrayed like one of these.
30 Wherefore, if God so clothe the grass of the field, which to day is, and to morrow is cast into the oven, shall he not much more clothe you, O ye of little faith?
31 Therefore take no thought, saying, What shall we eat? or, What shall we drink? or, Wherewithal shall we be clothed?
32 (For after all these things do the Gentiles seek:) for your heavenly Father knoweth that ye have need of all these things.
33 But seek ye first the kingdom of God, and his righteousness; and all these things shall be added unto you.
34 Take therefore no thought for the morrow: for the morrow shall take thought for the things of itself. Sufficient unto the day is the evil thereof.

Matthew 7:
1 Judge not, that ye be not judged.
2 For with what judgment ye judge, ye shall be judged: and with what measure ye mete, it shall be measured to you again.
3 And why beholdest thou the mote that is in thy brother's eye, but considerest not the beam that is in thine own eye?
4 Or how wilt thou say to thy brother, Let me pull out the mote out of thine eye; and, behold, a beam is in thine own eye?
5 Thou hypocrite, first cast out the beam out of thine own eye; and then shalt thou see clearly to cast out the mote out of thy brother's eye.
6 Give not that which is holy unto the dogs, neither cast ye your pearls before swine, lest they trample them under their feet, and turn again and rend you.
7 Ask, and it shall be given you; seek, and ye shall find; knock, and it shall be opened unto you:
8 For every one that asketh receiveth; and he that seeketh findeth; and to him that knocketh it shall be opened.
9 Or what man is there of you, whom if his son ask bread, will he give him a stone?
10 Or if he ask a fish, will he give him a serpent?
11 If ye then, being evil, know how to give good gifts unto your children, how much more shall your Father which is in heaven give good things to them that ask him?

12 Therefore all things whatsoever ye would that men should do to you, do ye even so to them: for this is the law and the prophets.
13 Enter ye in at the strait gate: for wide is the gate, and broad is the way, that leadeth to destruction, and many there be which go in thereat:
14 Because strait is the gate, and narrow is the way, which leadeth unto life, and few there be that find it.
15 Beware of false prophets, which come to you in sheep's clothing, but inwardly they are ravening wolves.
16 Ye shall know them by their fruits. Do men gather grapes of thorns, or figs of thistles?
17 Even so every good tree bringeth forth good fruit; but a corrupt tree bringeth forth evil fruit.
18 A good tree cannot bring forth evil fruit, neither can a corrupt tree bring forth good fruit.
19 Every tree that bringeth not forth good fruit is hewn down, and cast into the fire.
20 Wherefore by their fruits ye shall know them.
21 Not every one that saith unto me, Lord, Lord, shall enter into the kingdom of heaven; but he that doeth the will of my Father which is in heaven.
22 Many will say to me in that day, Lord, Lord, have we not prophesied in thy name? and in thy name have cast out devils? and in thy name done many wonderful works?
23 And then will I profess unto them, I never knew you: depart from me, ye that work iniquity.
24 Therefore whosoever heareth these sayings of mine, and doeth them, I will liken him unto a wise man, which built his house upon a rock:
25 And the rain descended, and the floods came, and the winds blew, and beat upon that house; and it fell not: for it was founded upon a rock.
26 And every one that heareth these sayings of mine, and doeth them not, shall be likened unto a foolish man, which built his house upon the sand:
27 And the rain descended, and the floods came, and the winds blew, and beat upon that house; and it fell: and great was the fall of it.
28 And it came to pass, when Jesus had ended these sayings, the people were astonished at his doctrine:
29 For he taught them as one having authority, and not as the scribes.

50 John 19:
30 When Jesus therefore had received the vinegar, he said, It is finished: and he bowed his head, and gave up the ghost.

51 Mark 7:
15 There is nothing from without a man, that entering into him can defile him: but the things which come out of him, those are they that defile the man.
16 If any man have ears to hear, let him hear.
17 And when he was entered into the house from the people, his disciples asked him concerning the parable.
18 And he saith unto them, Are ye so without understanding also? Do ye not perceive, that whatsoever thing from without entereth into the man, it cannot defile him;
19 Because it entereth not into his heart, but into the belly, and goeth out into the draught, purging all meats?
20 And he said, That which cometh out of the man, that defileth the man.
21 For from within, out of the heart of men, proceed evil thoughts, adulteries, fornications, murders,
22 Thefts, covetousness, wickedness, deceit, lasciviousness, an evil eye, blasphemy, pride, foolishness:
23 All these evil things come from within, and defile the man.

52 Matthew 12:
14 Then the Pharisees went out, and held a council against him, how they might destroy him.

53 Matthew 12:
22 Then was brought unto him one possessed with a devil, blind, and dumb: and he healed him, insomuch that the blind and dumb both spake and saw.
23 And all the people were amazed, and said, Is not this the son of David?
24 But when the Pharisees heard it, they said, This fellow doth not cast out devils, but by Beelzebub the prince of the devils.

25 And Jesus knew their thoughts, and said unto them, Every kingdom divided against itself is brought to desolation; and every city or house divided against itself shall not stand:
26 And if Satan cast out Satan, he is divided against himself; how shall then his kingdom stand?
27 And if I by Beelzebub cast out devils, by whom do your children cast them out? therefore they shall be your judges.
28 But if I cast out devils by the Spirit of God, then the kingdom of God is come unto you.
29 Or else how can one enter into a strong man's house, and spoil his goods, except he first bind the strong man? and then he will spoil his house.
30 He that is not with me is against me; and he that gathereth not with me scattereth abroad.
31 Wherefore I say unto you, All manner of sin and blasphemy shall be forgiven unto men: but the blasphemy against the Holy Ghost shall not be forgiven unto men.
32 And whosoever speaketh a word against the Son of man, it shall be forgiven him: but whosoever speaketh against the Holy Ghost, it shall not be forgiven him, neither in this world, neither in the world to come.

54 Matthew 21:
31 Whether of them twain did the will of his father? They say unto him, The first. Jesus saith unto them, Verily I say unto you, That the publicans and the harlots go into the kingdom of God before you.

9. Mark

55 Mark 11:
27 And they come again to Jerusalem: and as he was walking in the temple, there come to him the chief priests, and the scribes, and the elders,
28 And say unto him, By what authority doest thou these things? and who gave thee this authority to do these things?
29 And Jesus answered and said unto them, I will also ask of you one question, and answer me, and I will tell you by what authority I do these things.
30 The baptism of John, was it from heaven, or of men? answer me.
31 And they reasoned with themselves, saying, If we shall say, From heaven; he will say, Why then did ye not believe him?
32 But if we shall say, Of men; they feared the people: for all men counted John, that he was a prophet indeed.
33 And they answered and said unto Jesus, We cannot tell. And Jesus answering saith unto them, Neither do I tell you by what authority I do these things.
Mark 12:
1 And he began to speak unto them by parables. A certain man planted a vineyard, and set an hedge about it, and digged a place for the winefat, and built a tower, and let it out to husbandmen, and went into a far country.
2 And at the season he sent to the husbandmen a servant, that he might receive from the husbandmen of the fruit of the vineyard.
3 And they caught him, and beat him, and sent him away empty.
4 And again he sent unto them another servant; and at him they cast stones, and wounded him in the head, and sent him away shamefully handled.
5 And again he sent another; and him they killed, and many others; beating some, and killing some.
6 Having yet therefore one son, his wellbeloved, he sent him also last unto them, saying, They will reverence my son.
7 But those husbandmen said among themselves, This is the heir; come, let us kill him, and the inheritance shall be ours.
8 And they took him, and killed him, and cast him out of the vineyard.
9 What shall therefore the lord of the vineyard do? he will come and destroy the husbandmen, and will give the vineyard unto others.
10 And have ye not read this scripture; The stone which the builders rejected is become the head of the corner:
11 This was the Lord's doing, and it is marvellous in our eyes?

12 And they sought to lay hold on him, but feared the people: for they knew that he had spoken the parable against them: and they left him, and went their way.

56 Mark 12:
14 And when they were come, they say unto him, Master, we know that thou art true, and carest for no man: for thou regardest not the person of men, but teachest the way of God in truth: Is it lawful to give tribute to Caesar, or not?

57 Mark 12:
23 In the resurrection therefore, when they shall rise, whose wife shall she be of them? for the seven had her to wife.

58 Mark 12:
17 And Jesus answering said unto them, Render to Caesar the things that are Caesar's, and to God the things that are God's. And they marvelled at him.

59 Mark 12:
25 For when they shall rise from the dead, they neither marry, nor are given in marriage; but are as the angels which are in heaven.

60 John 1:
14 And the Word was made flesh, and dwelt among us, (and we beheld his glory, the glory as of the only begotten of the Father,) full of grace and truth.

10. Luke

62 Luke 2:
19 But Mary kept all these things, and pondered them in her heart.

63 Luke 2:
51 And he went down with them, and came to Nazareth, and was subject unto them: but his mother kept all these sayings in her heart.

11. Simmer to Boil

64 Luke 4:
30 But he passing through the midst of them went his way,

65 Isaiah 61:
1 The Spirit of the Lord GOD is upon me; because the LORD hath anointed me to preach good tidings unto the meek; he hath sent me to bind up the brokenhearted, to proclaim liberty to the captives, and the opening of the prison to them that are bound;
2 To proclaim the acceptable year of the LORD, and the day of vengeance of our God; to comfort all that mourn;

66 Luke 6:
11 And they were filled with madness; and communed one with another what they might do to Jesus.

67 John 10:
3 To him the porter openeth; and the sheep hear his voice: and he calleth his own sheep by name, and leadeth them out.
4 And when he putteth forth his own sheep, he goeth before them, and the sheep follow him: for they know his voice.
5 And a stranger will they not follow, but will flee from him: for they know not the voice of strangers.

References

68 John 2:
9 When the ruler of the feast had tasted the water that was made wine, and knew not whence it was: (but the servants which drew the water knew;) the governor of the feast called the bridegroom,

71 Acts 2:
13 Others mocking said, These men are full of new wine.

72 Acts 2:
15 For these are not drunken, as ye suppose, seeing it is but the third hour of the day.

73 Mark 2:
22 And no man putteth new wine into old bottles: else the new wine doth burst the bottles, and the wine is spilled, and the bottles will be marred: but new wine must be put into new bottles.

74 1 Timothy 4:
1 Now the Spirit speaketh expressly, that in the latter times some shall depart from the faith, giving heed to seducing spirits, and doctrines of devils;
2 Speaking lies in hypocrisy; having their conscience seared with a hot iron;
3 Forbidding to marry, and commanding to abstain from meats, which God hath created to be received with thanksgiving of them which believe and know the truth.
4 For every creature of God is good, and nothing to be refused, if it be received with thanksgiving:
5 For it is sanctified by the word of God and prayer.

75 1 Timothy 5:
23 Drink no longer water, but use a little wine for thy stomach's sake and thine often infirmities.

12. Boil

76 Matthew 27:
25 Then answered all the people, and said, His blood be on us, and on our children.

77 Acts 5:
28 Saying, Did not we straitly command you that ye should not teach in this name? and, behold, ye have filled Jerusalem with your doctrine, and intend to bring this man's blood upon us.

13. Yoke

78 Daniel 9:
24 Seventy weeks are determined upon thy people and upon thy holy city, to finish the transgression, and to make an end of sins, and to make reconciliation for iniquity, and to bring in everlasting righteousness, and to seal up the vision and prophecy, and to anoint the most Holy.
25 Know therefore and understand, that from the going forth of the commandment to restore and to build Jerusalem unto the Messiah the Prince shall be seven weeks, and threescore and two weeks: the street shall be built again, and the wall, even in troublous times.

79 Colossians 2:
15 And having spoiled principalities and powers, he made a shew of them openly, triumphing over them in it.

80 Luke 19:
11 And as they heard these things, he added and spake a parable, because he was nigh to Jerusalem, and because they thought that the kingdom of God should immediately appear.

81 John 2:

20 Then said the Jews, Forty and six years was this temple in building, and wilt thou rear it up in three days?

82 Matthew 13:
55 Is not this the carpenter's son? is not his mother called Mary? and his brethren, James, and Joses, and Simon, and Judas?

14. SuperMan

84 John 19:
19 And Pilate wrote a title, and put it on the cross. And the writing was, JESUS OF NAZARETH THE KING OF THE JEWS.

85 John 1:
1 In the beginning was the Word, and the Word was with God, and the Word was God.

1 John 1:
14 And the Word was made flesh, and dwelt among us, (and we beheld his glory, the glory as of the only begotten of the Father,) full of grace and truth.

87 2 Corinthians 3:
6
Who also hath made us able ministers of the new testament; not of the letter, but of the spirit: for the letter killeth, but the spirit giveth life.
7 But if the ministration of death, written and engraven in stones, was glorious, so that the children of Israel could not stedfastly behold the face of Moses for the glory of his countenance; which glory was to be done away:

88 Romans 4:
15 Because the law worketh wrath: for where no law is, there is no transgression.

89 Ephesians 6:
12 For we wrestle not against flesh and blood, but against principalities, against powers, against the rulers of the darkness of this world, against spiritual wickedness in high places.

91 Colossians 3:
9 Lie not one to another, seeing that ye have put off the old man with his deeds;

94 2 Corinthians 2:
11 Lest Satan should get an advantage of us: for we are not ignorant of his devices.

95 Genesis 1:
28 And God blessed them, and God said unto them, Be fruitful, and multiply, and replenish the earth, and subdue it: and have dominion over the fish of the sea, and over the fowl of the air, and over every living thing that moveth upon the earth.

96 Genesis 3:
7 And the eyes of them both were opened, and they knew that they were naked; and they sewed fig leaves together, and made themselves aprons.

97 Romans 6:
16 Know ye not, that to whom ye yield yourselves servants to obey, his servants ye are to whom ye obey; whether of sin unto death, or of obedience unto righteousness?

15. Supermen

98 John 3:

References

3 Jesus answered and said unto him, Verily, verily, I say unto thee, Except a man be born again, he cannot see the kingdom of God.

99 1 Peter 1:
10 Of which salvation the prophets have enquired and searched diligently, who prophesied of the grace that should come unto you:
11 Searching what, or what manner of time the Spirit of Christ which was in them did signify, when it testified beforehand the sufferings of Christ, and the glory that should follow.
12 Unto whom it was revealed, that not unto themselves, but unto us they did minister the things, which are now reported unto you by them that have preached the gospel unto you with the Holy Ghost sent down from heaven; which things the angels desire to look into.

100 Genesis 2:
17 But of the tree of the knowledge of good and evil, thou shalt not eat of it: for in the day that thou eatest thereof thou shalt surely die.

101 Genesis 5:
5 And all the days that Adam lived were nine hundred and thirty years: and he died.

102 Psalm 90:
4 For a thousand years in thy sight are but as yesterday when it is past, and as a watch in the night.

2 Peter 3:
8 But, beloved, be not ignorant of this one thing, that one day is with the Lord as a thousand years, and a thousand years as one day.

103 Ephesians 2:
1 And you hath he quickened, who were dead in trespasses and sins;

Colossians 2:
13 And you, being dead in your sins and the uncircumcision of your flesh, hath he quickened together with him, having forgiven you all trespasses;

104 1 Corinthians 3:
16 Know ye not that ye are the temple of God, and that the Spirit of God dwelleth in you?

Ephesians 5:
18 And be not drunk with wine, wherein is excess; but be filled with the Spirit;

2 Timothy 1:
14 That good thing which was committed unto thee keep by the Holy Ghost which dwelleth in us.

1 John 4:
13 Hereby know we that we dwell in him, and he in us, because he hath given us of his Spirit.

105 John 3:
16 For God so loved the world, that he gave his only begotten Son, that whosoever believeth in him should not perish, but have everlasting life.

106 Matthew 28:
18 And Jesus came and spake unto them, saying, All power is given unto me in heaven and in earth.
19 Go ye therefore, and teach all nations, baptizing them in the name of the Father, and of the Son, and of the Holy Ghost:
20 Teaching them to observe all things whatsoever I have commanded you: and, lo, I am with you alway, even unto the end of the world. Amen.

Mark 16:
15 And he said unto them, Go ye into all the world, and preach the gospel to every creature.

16 He that believeth and is baptized shall be saved; but he that believeth not shall be damned.
17 And these signs shall follow them that believe; In my name shall they cast out devils; they shall speak with new tongues;
18 They shall take up serpents; and if they drink any deadly thing, it shall not hurt them; they shall lay hands on the sick, and they shall recover.

107 John 8:
44 Ye are of your father the devil, and the lusts of your father ye will do. He was a murderer from the beginning, and abode not in the truth, because there is no truth in him. When he speaketh a lie, he speaketh of his own: for he is a liar, and the father of it.

2 John 1:
7 For many deceivers are entered into the world, who confess not that Jesus Christ is come in the flesh. This is a deceiver and an antichrist.

108 Romans 13:
3 For rulers are not a terror to good works, but to the evil. Wilt thou then not be afraid of the power? do that which is good, and thou shalt have praise of the same:
4 For he is the minister of God to thee for good. But if thou do that which is evil, be afraid; for he beareth not the sword in vain: for he is the minister of God, a revenger to execute wrath upon him that doeth evil.

109 John 18:
36 Jesus answered, My kingdom is not of this world: if my kingdom were of this world, then would my servants fight, that I should not be delivered to the Jews: but now is my kingdom not from hence.

16. Stealth

111 Matthew 20:
20 Then came to him the mother of Zebedee's children with her sons, worshipping him, and desiring a certain thing of him.

112 Mark 10:
35 And James and John, the sons of Zebedee, come unto him, saying, Master, we would that thou shouldest do for us whatsoever we shall desire.
36 And he said unto them, What would ye that I should do for you?
37 They said unto him, Grant unto us that we may sit, one on thy right hand, and the other on thy left hand, in thy glory.

113 John 12:
6 This he said, not that he cared for the poor; but because he was a thief, and had the bag, and bare what was put therein.

17. Tough Guys

114 Matthew 26:
7 There came unto him a woman having an alabaster box of very precious ointment, and poured it on his head, as he sat at meat.

Mark 14:3
3 And being in Bethany in the house of Simon the leper, as he sat at meat, there came a woman having an alabaster box of ointment of spikenard very precious; and she brake the box, and poured it on his head.

Luke 7:
37 And, behold, a woman in the city, which was a sinner, when she knew that Jesus sat at meat in the Pharisee's house, brought an alabaster box of ointment,

115 John 20:

19 Then the same day at evening, being the first day of the week, when the doors were shut where the disciples were assembled for fear of the Jews, came Jesus and stood in the midst, and saith unto them, Peace be unto you.116 Acts 2:41

117 Acts 4:
4 Howbeit many of them which heard the word believed; and the number of the men was about five thousand.

118 Acts 6:
8 And Stephen, full of faith and power, did great wonders and miracles among the people.

119 Acts 6:
10 And they were not able to resist the wisdom and the spirit by which he spake.

120 Exodus 25:
9 According to all that I shew thee, after the pattern of the tabernacle, and the pattern of all the instruments thereof, even so shall ye make it.

121 1 Chronicles 28:
18 And for the altar of incense refined gold by weight; and gold for the pattern of the chariot of the cherubims, that spread out their wings, and covered the ark of the covenant of the LORD.
19 All this, said David, the LORD made me understand in writing by his hand upon me, even all the works of this pattern.

122 John 19:
19 When Jesus therefore had received the vinegar, he said, It is finished: and he bowed his head, and gave up the ghost.

123 Hebrews 9:
22 And almost all things are by the law purged with blood; and without shedding of blood is no remission.
23 It was therefore necessary that the patterns of things in the heavens should be purified with these; but the heavenly things themselves with better sacrifices than these.
24 For Christ is not entered into the holy places made with hands, which are the figures of the true; but into heaven itself, now to appear in the presence of God for us:
25 Nor yet that he should offer himself often, as the high priest entereth into the holy place every year with blood of others;
26 For then must he often have suffered since the foundation of the world: but now once in the end of the world hath he appeared to put away sin by the sacrifice of himself.
27 And as it is appointed unto men once to die, but after this the judgment:
28 So Christ was once offered to bear the sins of many; and unto them that look for him shall he appear the second time without sin unto salvation.

124 Hebrews 8:
1 Now of the things which we have spoken this is the sum: We have such an high priest, who is set on the right hand of the throne of the Majesty in the heavens;

Hebrews 10:
12 But this man, after he had offered one sacrifice for sins for ever, sat down on the right hand of God;

Hebrews 12:
2 Looking unto Jesus the author and finisher of our faith; who for the joy that was set before him endured the cross, despising the shame, and is set down at the right hand of the throne of God.

18. Saul

125 Acts 12:
1 Now about that time Herod the king stretched forth his hands to vex certain of the church.
2 And he killed James the brother of John with the sword.

126 Acts 12:
3 And because he saw it pleased the Jews, he proceeded further to take Peter also. (Then were the days of unleavened bread.)

127 Acts 12:
7 And, behold, the angel of the Lord came upon him, and a light shined in the prison: and he smote Peter on the side, and raised him up, saying, Arise up quickly. And his chains fell off from his hands.
8 And the angel said unto him, Gird thyself, and bind on thy sandals. And so he did. And he saith unto him, Cast thy garment about thee, and follow me.
9 And he went out, and followed him; and wist not that it was true which was done by the angel; but thought he saw a vision.
10 When they were past the first and the second ward, they came unto the iron gate that leadeth unto the city; which opened to them of his own accord: and they went out, and passed on through one street; and forthwith the angel departed from him.
11 And when Peter was come to himself, he said, Now I know of a surety, that the Lord hath sent his angel, and hath delivered me out of the hand of Herod, and from all the expectation of the people of the Jews.

130 1 Corinthians 15:
9 For I am the least of the apostles, that am not meet to be called an apostle, because I persecuted the church of God.

131 Acts 17:
5 But the Jews which believed not, moved with envy, took unto them certain lewd fellows of the baser sort, and gathered a company, and set all the city on an uproar, and assaulted the house of Jason, and sought to bring them out to the people.
6 And when they found them not, they drew Jason and certain brethren unto the rulers of the city, crying, These that have turned the world upside down are come hither also;
7 Whom Jason hath received: and these all do contrary to the decrees of Caesar, saying that there is another king, one Jesus.
8 And they troubled the people and the rulers of the city, when they heard these things.
9 And when they had taken security of Jason, and of the other, they let them go.

132 Acts 19:
21 After these things were ended, Paul purposed in the spirit, when he had passed through Macedonia and Achaia, to go to Jerusalem, saying, After I have been there, I must also see Rome.
22 So he sent into Macedonia two of them that ministered unto him, Timotheus and Erastus; but he himself stayed in Asia for a season.
23 And the same time there arose no small stir about that way.
24 For a certain man named Demetrius, a silversmith, which made silver shrines for Diana, brought no small gain unto the craftsmen;
25 Whom he called together with the workmen of like occupation, and said, Sirs, ye know that by this craft we have our wealth.
26 Moreover ye see and hear, that not alone at Ephesus, but almost throughout all Asia, this Paul hath persuaded and turned away much people, saying that they be no gods, which are made with hands:
27 So that not only this our craft is in danger to be set at nought; but also that the temple of the great goddess Diana should be despised, and her magnificence should be destroyed, whom all Asia and the world worshippeth.
28 And when they heard these sayings, they were full of wrath, and cried out, saying, Great is Diana of the Ephesians.
29 And the whole city was filled with confusion: and having caught Gaius and Aristarchus, men of Macedonia, Paul's companions in travel, they rushed with one accord into the theatre.
30 And when Paul would have entered in unto the people, the disciples suffered him not.
31 And certain of the chief of Asia, which were his friends, sent unto him, desiring him that he would not adventure himself into the theatre.
32 Some therefore cried one thing, and some another: for the assembly was confused; and the more part knew not wherefore they were come together.

33 And they drew Alexander out of the multitude, the Jews putting him forward. And Alexander beckoned with the hand, and would have made his defence unto the people.
34 But when they knew that he was a Jew, all with one voice about the space of two hours cried out, Great is Diana of the Ephesians.
35 And when the townclerk had appeased the people, he said, Ye men of Ephesus, what man is there that knoweth not how that the city of the Ephesians is a worshipper of the great goddess Diana, and of the image which fell down from Jupiter?
36 Seeing then that these things cannot be spoken against, ye ought to be quiet, and to do nothing rashly.
37 For ye have brought hither these men, which are neither robbers of churches, nor yet blasphemers of your goddess.
38 Wherefore if Demetrius, and the craftsmen which are with him, have a matter against any man, the law is open, and there are deputies: let them implead one another.
39 But if ye enquire any thing concerning other matters, it shall be determined in a lawful assembly.
40 For we are in danger to be called in question for this day's uproar, there being no cause whereby we may give an account of this concourse.
41 And when he had thus spoken, he dismissed the assembly.

133 Romans 12:
2 And be not conformed to this world: but be ye transformed by the renewing of your mind, that ye may prove what is that good, and acceptable, and perfect, will of God.

134 Romans 8:
29 For whom he did foreknow, he also did predestinate to be conformed to the image of his Son, that he might be the firstborn among many brethren.

19. Return

135 Luke 3:
21 Now when all the people were baptized, it came to pass, that Jesus also being baptized, and praying, the heaven was opened,
22 And the Holy Ghost descended in a bodily shape like a dove upon him, and a voice came from heaven, which said, Thou art my beloved Son; in thee I am well pleased.
23 And Jesus himself began to be about thirty years of age, being (as was supposed) the son of Joseph, which was the son of Heli,

136 Luke 4:
1 And Jesus being full of the Holy Ghost returned from Jordan, and was led by the Spirit into the wilderness,
2 Being forty days tempted of the devil. And in those days he did eat nothing: and when they were ended, he afterward hungered.

www.ingramcontent.com/pod-product-compliance
Lightning Source LLC
Chambersburg PA
CBHW070620050426
42450CB00011B/3084